Me the People

Lisa Fontana

Me The People
By Lisa Fontana

ISBN-13: 978-1535283076
ISBN-10: 1535283076

Design, Layout, and Typesetting by Alexander Becker
www.alexanderbecker.net

Contents

Introduction

"Why do politicians always tell us to write our congressman? What does that even mean??"

"If I'm not part of the solution, I'm part of the problem? Ummm, the solution to what?"

"Ya know, those Rock the Vote commercials are cute, but then what? Rock the vote how? By doing what? Going where?"

"I watch the news sometimes. The reporters and the politicians are all so negative and angry. I end up upset, overwhelmed or more confused than before, so why bother?"

"Maybe I am embarrassingly uninformed. I do care. I just don't know how to change it."

Start playing sappy music from a TV commercial in your head and then read:

There is an age when it's no longer okay to be ignorant of our political system; no longer okay that you haven't voted or don't even know how to register. No one knows the age, but we all know that once we've passed it we are alone, unable to broadcast our ignorance even if we wanted to change it, because we know we'll be judged or ridiculed for being un-American. We feel unwanted and unwelcome. If you have found yourself in this situation remember one thing (Now change the music to the upbeat, flag-waving variety):

"You are not alone, it is changeable, and the opinions of those people don't matter."

Everyone who has ever judged or ridiculed you for what you do not know is behaving like the true Un-American... and is a bad-mannered numbskull who probably ate paste during nap time and never ever learned to share their toys!!

However they got to where they are today, many people 'in the know' don't understand why you and I didn't get to the same place; which is politically aware, politically involved and governmentally savvy. If they could, rather than tearing us down and blaming us for being 'the problem,' they might choose to extend a hand and bring us along in the process.

Forget about them for a while, because our situation is really pretty simple. We can't grow if we don't learn and we can't learn if we won't admit what we don't know. I believe that the truest meaning of government is 'the way we are together.' So if you are interested in growing in this area, I invite you to join me in sticking out your tongue at those who would shame us for our 'ignorance,' and then let's grow a little together.

Main Goal

Government exists on three levels: Local, state and national. This guide focuses on the National level, with the goal of providing the tools to help you decide on and then vote for the next president of the United States of America. It is my hope that you will learn, choose, and share.

- **Learn** as much as you need to so you can involve yourself as much (or as little) as you want.

- **Choose** your candidate and cast your vote.

- **Share** this information in some capacity with one other person so this awareness can grow.

Who am I?

I am an average American. I am college educated and I own a small business... I was also 35 years old when I first voted for the president. Oddly, I cast my first vote the same year I was legally eligible to run for the job! I tried to buy a book to teach me about politics or government so I could vote with confidence, but the bookstore shelves were lined with negativity, blame and straight up hate. The few helpful books I came across were either incomplete or beyond me.

I couldn't ask anyone for help because it hadn't gone well in the past. On a personal dare, I told 17 people in one day that I had never voted before. All 17 reacted as if I'd confessed to drowning puppies in their sleep. Not one of them offered me anything but their frustration with my stupidity and apathy. So, I decided to quietly put some pieces together on my own, and now I am sharing what I learned with anyone else who might be looking for it too.

My Promise

I promise to keep it cheerful and short. I will try to make you smile, and I will not make you frown. I will try to make you feel welcome and wanted, and I promise this is, and will remain, a judgement-free zone. And if you end up not voting at all, I will not call you stupid and I will not call you un-American. Most of all I promise it will be fun, easy and balanced. The way all great things in life should be.

Me The People

Registering is a Piece of Cake

So, you want to register to vote? GREAT. Let's run through the Who, What, Where When, Why, and How:

What is voting? A formal expression of your opinion or your choice.

What does it mean to register? To put yourself on an official list of people who can vote.

Who can vote? Every American citizen 18 years of age or older (unless you have been convicted of a felony, which varies by state, or have been declared mentally incompetent). Dates for Primaries and Caucuses vary by state.

Primaries and Caucuses: Methods that political parties use to select candidates for a general election. (more on these later).

When Do I vote? The date of the next General Election is Tuesday, November 8, 2016, and future elections will be held every four years on the first Tuesday in November.

How long do I have to register? That depends on the state you live in. In Illinois, for example, the last day to register to vote is October 11, 2016, while in Delaware, it's October 15, 2016. I recommend you register immediately to avoid disappointment. To find out the registration deadline date in your state go to **www.Vote411.org**, then click on '**Your Voting Guide**.' Type in your street address, city, state and zip code.

Where **do I register and** *What* **is the process?** Every state has different locations where you may register to vote:

- County Clerk's Office
- Board of election commissioner's office
- City and Village Offices
- Township Offices
- Deputy Registrars
- Public Libraries
- Military Recruitment Offices
- Offices that offer public assistance

9

The most common way is to go to your local DMV (**D**epartment of **M**otor **V**ehicles). Thanks to the *"Motor Voter"* law, all citizens in every state can register to vote there. I know DMV workers don't always have the best reputation for being helpful, but they will register you to vote and that is what you want. If you've had a bad experience at the DMV in the past, maybe bring a friend along for some cheery conversation while you wait.

This law also allows you to mail in your voter registration, so if the DMV is not for you, go online and print one out. The site I recommend is **www.vote411.org**. Click on **'Register to Vote.'** You will be walked through the process and they will email you a registration form. Print it out, fill it out and mail it out. You can also use it to update registration information due to a change of name or address, and to switch or register with a political party, or to register to vote. If you prefer to go low tech, you may pick up an application from many of the locations listed above. If you want to go super low tech and stay home, a registration form can be found in most telephone books.

FYI – Depending on the rules of your state, if you choose to register by mail you may have to vote in person the first time you vote. This means you won't be able to do an absentee ballot. Once your voter's registration card arrives in the mail however, you can still vote early (more on these later).

Absentee Ballot: A ballot submitted by mail before an election by a voter who is unable to come to the polls in person.

Ballot: A process of voting in writing, and typically in secret.

State Election Office/State Board of Elections: A body designated to conduct elections in a state.

Early Voting: The process by which electors can vote on a single or series of days prior to an election. It can take place remotely, such as by mail, or in person, usually in designated early voting polling places.

An exception to Mail-In Registration: A few states do not accept MAIL-IN voter registration forms; which means that you must register in person. The states that are exempt from "Motor Voter" include: (Minnesota, Montana, North Dakota, Wyoming, Wisconsin, Idaho, Maine and New Hampshire). This is because they either allow Americans to register on Election Day at the polls or, (and this only applies to North Dakota), registration is not required.

Do I have to register with a political party when I register to vote? No. You are free to simply register. Some states require you to declare a party (*I am a Democrat. I am a Republican. I am an Independent*) in order to vote in the primary election or caucus (Which is the preliminary election to select the party candidates who will run in the general election. If this is confusing, no worries: more on this later.).

Ballots Scare Me

Me too! While it is true that you will be presented with a whole bunch more to vote on than just the president, don't sweat it. First, if you only vote for the person you want to be president and then turn in an otherwise blank ballot, your vote counts. Second, you can easily get a copy of the ballot before Election Day, so there won't be any surprises. There will be more later on the additional 'stuff' you might be asked to vote for in your state and city, but getting an early copy will allow you to sit at your kitchen table in a "no pressure" environment and decide who all you plan to vote for. To do this, all you need is to contact the County Clerk at your **State Election Office**, also called **State Board of Elections.** Ask them for a sample copy of the ballot. NOTE: If you are feeling overwhelmed by this, no worries – you can do this online (low tech: You can walk into your local public library and ask for help at the front desk).

Find Your Local Election Office Online

Go to **www.votesmart.org.** Scroll to the bottom of the home page and under **ELECTIONS & CANDIDATES** click on '**Election Contacts**' and select your state. A list of local offices will pop up and you can find the web address, street address, phone number and email of your county's election office. If you don't 'do' the web, you can make a stop at your local library. Tell them you would like to find the phone number and contact information of the County Clerk's Office for your county.

How can I vote on a Tuesday when I work on Tuesday? Most companies give their employees time to go vote. Polling opens pretty early in the morning and closes pretty late at night (exact times depend on your state), which should allow you enough time to go to your designated polling place and vote. Why not vote early and skip the long lines and the last minute hoopla? Approximately thirty-two states (& the District of Columbia – which is Washington D.C.) allow some form of early voting at designated early polling places. Contact your local election official or **www.LongDistanceVoter.org** to find out about early voting in your state.

Polling Place: A building where voting takes place during an election.

Everything Else: If you have additional questions about anything voting related, go back to the **www.Vote411.org** homepage. Click on the box marked **Search by State and Topic**. There you will find information on topics such as:

- Absentee Voting
- Candidate & Ballot Measures Information
- Early Voting
- Election Dates
- Eligibility Requirements
- ID Requirements
- Poll Workers
- Polling Place Details
- Provisional Voting
- Voter Registration
- Voting Machines

Fun Fact: Many people believe that if they don't register to vote they will be spared Jury Duty. That is an Urban Myth. If you have a license to drive or a state ID it's only a matter of time before a summons comes your way. Even Donald Trump gets called to Jury Duty, so pack a book, a snack and a patriotic smile.

Parting Words on Voting: The U.S. Department of Transportation estimates that 6-12% of voters do not have a government-issued photo ID: Driver's license, state ID, etc. We assume all American citizens possess this kind of official identification, but people who were born outside of hospitals may have a hard time obtaining birth certificates or other proof of citizenship. The groups affected are primarily young people, the poor, people of color, and senior citizens. We all deserve to have our vote count. If this topic interests you, you might want to learn more about the NVRA (National Voter Registration Act of 1983) or Motor Voter Act.

Congrats! Now you can be an official, registered voter!

What's Next?

If you want to know a little about the government, we should visit the coolest tree house ever! Get ready to cheer like a kid and swing like a monkey, 'cuz nothing is more fun than…

Me The People

Climbing the Tree of the Three Branches of Government

The easiest way to learn anything new is to sit on a playground and think like a child. Books for kids, shows for kids, recordings for kids! The absolute best way to learn anything new that you are confused or intimidated by is through information designed for children. It is simply and enthusiastically broken down to both teach and excite. So when it comes to learning about the three branches of government you can't beat the *Schoolhouse Rock! America Rock!* collection of videos to gain a sense of how the government works and how you and I fit into it. These DVD's are short, fun, and easily ordered from Amazon, or checked out through your local library. With donkeys, elephants and lame ducks to parade around it's no wonder they compare the three branches of government to a three ring circus.

Donkey: This animal represents the Democratic party.

Elephant: This animal represents the Republican party.

Lame Duck: When the current president either loses the election to stay in office or is coming to the end of the second term, then he/she is only president for a couple more months before 'the new guy' takes over. Lame Duck refers to that time period.

These branches were put in place by the framers as a check and balance to prevent an abuse of power. Separate and independent powers and areas of responsibility were assigned to each of the three so that no one branch would have more than the other two. Prepare to scrape your knuckles and rip a hole in your jeans as we climb the tree of the three branches!

The Framers: This title refers to the men who put together the U.S. Constitution.

Branch Number One – The Executive

The branch of the United States government that is responsible for implementing and enforcing the laws written by Congress. The power of this branch lies with the President of the United States, who also acts as Head of State and Commander-in-Chief of the armed forces. The president appoints the heads of the federal agencies, including the Cabinet. The Vice President is also part of the Executive Branch.

Congress: The legislative body of the U.S.

Legislative: Having power to make the laws.

The President of the United States: Head of the Executive Branch. The president's power is dictated by the Constitution.

Head of State: The chief public representative of a country who may also be the head of the government.

Head of Government: Describes either the highest or second highest official in the executive branch of a sovereign state, a federated state, or a self-governing colony who often presides over a cabinet.

Commander-in-Chief: A head of state or officer in supreme command of a country's military.

The Vice President of the United States: Is the first person in the presidential line of succession, becoming the new President of the United States upon the death, resignation, or removal of the president.

The Cabinet: Is traditionally made up of the Vice President and the heads of 15 executive departments. Their job is to advise the president on any subject he/she may require relating to the duties of their respective offices. Some of these include the Department of Defense, the Department of Agriculture, and the Department of the Interior.

Fun Fact: According to the White House, including members of the armed forces, the Executive Branch employs more than 4 million people.

Funner Fact: The framers made sure that the Executive Branch was the weakest of the three branches because we were breaking off from the royalist model (kings and queens) that put absolute power in the hands of just one person.

Branch Number Two – The Legislative

The Branch of the United States government that is made up of the House of Representatives and the Senate. The legislative branch is bicameral and together they form the Congress. The Constitution grants Congress the sole authority to pass laws and declare war, the right to confirm or reject many Presidential appointments, and great power to investigate things.

The reason there are two groups is because the framers wanted checks and balances. In the House of Representatives the people are elected by and represented by many different districts of each state, which means they should have a strong understanding of how laws and changes in the government will affect the small group of people they represent. The members of the Senate are elected by everyone in their state, and they make decisions based on the nation as a whole. The goal is to make decisions that do the most good locally and globally.

Bicameral: Made up of 2 chambers.

Chamber: A legislative, judicial, or other like body.

Congress: Is the national legislative body (the people who make the laws) and is made up of the Senate and the House of Representatives.

Checks and Balances: A system that allows each branch of a government to change or veto acts of another branch to prevent any one branch from becoming too powerful.

Districts: States are divided into sections of territory. Each section is permitted one U.S. Congressperson to represent the people in that section in the U.S. House of Representatives.

Chamber 1

The House of Representatives is made up of 435 elected members called Congressmen/women (or Representatives), and are divided among the 50 states according to population. In addition, there are 6 non-voting members, representing the District of Columbia, the Commonwealth of Puerto Rico, and four other territories of the United States. The person who is in charge of the chamber is the Speaker of the House. This person will be one of the 435 members and is elected by the Representatives. The powers assigned to the House include the power to start revenue bills, impeach federal officials, and elect the president in the case of an Electoral College tie.

Congressmen/women: Members of the House of Representatives who were elected by a district in their state. Their job is to make laws, and they serve a 2 year term. They are also called Representatives.

Revenue: Income.

Impeach: A process that is used to charge, try, and remove public officials for misconduct while in office.

District: Each state is divided into areas called districts.

Chamber 2

The Senate Is made up of 100 Senators, 2 per state. The Senate has sole power to confirm any appointments made by the president (if they require consent), and to ratify treaties. There are, however, two exceptions to this rule: the House of Representatives must also approve appointments to the Vice Presidency and any treaty that involves foreign trade. The Senate also tries impeachment cases for federal officials referred to it by the House of Representatives.

Senators: Members of the Senate who were elected by their state. Their job is to make laws, and they serve 6 year terms.

Ratify: To make something legal by signing it or giving formal consent.

Treaties: A formal agreement between two or more states.

How it Works

In order to pass legislation and send it to the president for a signature, both the House and the Senate must pass the same bill by majority vote. If the president vetoes a bill, they may override the veto by passing the bill again in each chamber with at least two-thirds of each body voting in favor.

Veto: A vote that blocks a decision made by law makers.

Fun Fact: The Vice President of the United States serves as President of the Senate and may cast the deciding vote there in the event of a tie.

Funner Fact: The framers called the Legislative branch the People's Branch, and designed it to be the most powerful.

Branch Number Three – The Judicial

This is the branch of the United States government responsible for the administration of justice. The job of this branch is to interpret the law. Headed by the Supreme Court, its powers include interpreting the Constitution, reviewing laws, and deciding cases involving states' rights.

Fun Fact: All Justices are nominated by the president, confirmed by the Senate, and they get to keep their jobs until they die unless they resign, or are impeached and convicted by Congress.

Me The People

A Little Bit More

Job Descriptions for Key Positions in **Government**

The three branches are the basic building blocks of our government. They work together, which means the presidential candidate you vote for will need to play well with others. Knowing more about the jobs held by the people in these three branches will help you see where you want to place your expectations. It can feel like a lot to take in, so you if you want to take a break and skip ahead to the History Sprint, please do. Just remember to stretch first.

Executive Branch

Duties of The President of the United States

- Commander in Chief of the Armed Forces
- Make Treaties
- Receive ambassadors and other public ministers from foreign countries
- Appoint ambassadors, Supreme Court justices, federal judges, and any officials as provided for by the Congress, with the approval of the Senate
- Give an annual State of the Union Address to Congress
- Propose new laws
- Sign bills into law and veto bills
- Protect and defend the laws of the United States
- Convene Congress on extraordinary occasions
- Adjourn Congress, in cases of a disagreement about adjournment
- Take care that the laws be faithfully executed
- Grant Reprieves and pardons for offenses against the U.S.

Appoint: To assign a job or a role.

Propose: To put forward an idea or plan for consideration.

Convene: To call people together.

Adjourn: Stop a meeting with the intention of coming back to it later.

Limits of Power

The president has the power to appoint ambassadors to other countries, but only with approval from the Senate.

While the president can authorize the use of troops overseas without declaring war, Congress must approve it if he/she wants to officially 'declare war.'

The president meets with the leaders of other countries, has the power to recognize those lands as official countries and is allowed to make treaties with them. No treaty is official, however, until it is approved by the Senate.

Yes, the head of each department in the Executive Branch is appointed by the president, but appointments are subject to the approval of the Senate.

Perks

The president gets to ride around in Air Force One, makes $400,000, has a $50,000 expense account, plus free room and board.

Duties of the Vice President of the United States

The primary function of this person is to be first in the presidential line of succession, should the president die, resign or be removed from office during his or her term in office. As outlined by the Constitution of the United States, the vice president also serves as the President of the Senate, and may break tie votes in that chamber.

Limits of Power

He or she may be assigned additional duties by the president, but the Constitution assigns no executive powers to the vice president, so in performing those duties would be acting only as an agent of the president.

Duties of the Cabinet

The head of each department advises the president on any subject he/she may require relating to the duties of their own offices.

The Cabinet is made up of:

Department of Education: Focuses on ensuring equal access to education, and promotes excellence in education.

Homeland Security: Is supposed to prevent terrorist attacks on U.S. soil.

Department of Housing and Urban Development: Was created to apply programs that offer help for housing and for the development of communities.

Department Veteran Affairs: Handles programs for veterans and their families.

Department of Energy: Provides technical information and the scientific and educational foundation for the technology, policy and leadership to achieve efficiency in energy use and diversity in sources.

Department of Transportation: Establishes the Nation's overall transportation policy, such as highway planning, mass transit, railroads, aviation and more.

Department of Health and Human Services: Focuses on health and welfare, and is basically people serving people.

Department of Labor: Promotes and develops the welfare of U.S. wage earners, to improve their working conditions, and to advance their opportunities for gainful jobs.

Department of Commerce: Supports, serves, and promotes the Nation's international trade, economic growth, and advancement in technology.

Department of Agriculture: Mainly focuses on improving and maintaining farm income, as well as enhancing the environment and helping landowners protect soil, water and other natural resources.

Department of Justice: Provides counsel of American citizens and represents them in enforcing the law in the public interest.

Department of State: Advises the President in formulating and executing foreign policy and promoting the long-term security and well-being of the United States.

Department of the Interior: Protects and provides access to the Nation's natural and cultural heritage, as well as honor trust responsibilities to tribes.

Department of Defense: Responsible for providing the military forces needed to deter war and protect the security of our country.

Department of Treasury: Has four basic functions: Creating and recommending economic financial, tax, and fiscal policies; serving as financial agent for the U.S. Government; enforcing the law; and manufacturing money (paper and coin).

International Trade: The exchange of goods or services along international borders.

Economic Growth: An increase in the ability of an economy to produce goods and services, compared from one period of time to another.

Economy: Wealth and resources in terms of the production and consumption of goods and services.

Fiscal Policies: A government course of action for dealing with the budget (particularly with taxation and borrowing).

Legislative Branch

Duties of Congressmen and Congresswomen:

- Create laws that require people to pay taxes
- Decide whether or not a government official should be put on trial at the Senate for a crime against the country (impeachment)
- Serve 2 years

The Speaker of the House of Representatives: This person, called Speaker of the House, is the presiding officer of the House of Representatives.

Duties:

- Establishes the legislative agenda
- Maintains order within the house
- Presides over debate
- Appoints members of certain committees
- Administers the oath of office to House members
- This person is second in the line of presidential succession, behind the Vice President

Preside: Be in charge of or be in the position of authority in a meeting or gathering.

Duties of the Senators

- Accept or reject any treaties the president makes

- Confirm or deny anyone the president recommends for appointed jobs, such as cabinet officers and Supreme Court Justices

- Empowered to hold a trial for a government official accused of a crime against the country

President Pro Tempore: Commonly referred to as the President Pro-tem, this person is a Senator, usually the senior member of the majority party, who is chosen to preside over the Senate in the absence of the vice president. The President Pro Tempore is third in the line of presidential succession, behind the Vice President and the Speaker.

Duties:

- Rule on points of order
- Be one of the two authorities (The speaker is the other) to whom declarations of the President's ability or inability to resume the presidency must be approved by
- Appointment of various congressional officers, certain commissions, advisory boards, and committees

Senate Minority Leader and the Senate Majority Leader

They are elected by their party and are the chief Senate spokespeople for those parties. Each is elected to this position, and the Majority Leader is the Senator whose party has the most members, while the Minority Leader is the Senator whose party has the least.

Duties of Majority Leader

- Manage and schedule the legislative and executive business of the Senate
- Chief representative of the Senate

Perks:

Congressmen/women and Senators enjoy a base pay of $174,000. Great health insurance benefits, as well as an allowance to hire a full staff for all of their work needs in both their Washington and District offices. (If I had that kind of budget I think I'd hire a chef, a personal assistant and 24 hour maid service!)

Judicial Branch

There are nine Justices. They sit on the Supreme Court and their job is to decide cases that may or may not violate the Constitution. This process is called *Judicial Review*. Of the nine, one is the Chief Justice, and he or she is the head of the US federal court system. This person typically has the most seniority. These jobs are lifetime appointments and can only be lost by resigning, choosing to retire, dying, or by being impeached.

Duties of the Chief Justice

- Serve as the head of the federal judiciary

- Preside over impeachment trials of the president Impeachment trials

- Chair the conferences where cases are discussed and voted on by the justices

- Set the agenda for the weekly meetings where the justices review petitions to have a case heard by them

- Administer the oath of office at the inauguration of the President of the United States – however this is a tradition, not a constitutional responsibility

Political Parties: I'll buy the chips if you bring the dip!

Political parties are far less festive than they sound. For starters, there's no cake! ...and also... well, no party to go to. Before we explore political parties, a few background definitions might be helpful.

Politic: Shrewd or prudent in practical matters; tactful, diplomatic.

Use Politic in a sentence: At Dinner Jan's boyfriend told an offensive joke, but I found it more politic to hold my tongue than to call him on it.

Politics: The science or art of government. It is also the name of the profession of performing the science or art of government.

Use Politics in a sentence: We only went to Jan's house so we could relax and hang out, but her boyfriend works in politics, so that's all they talked about the whole time.

Government: The way we are together. A body that makes and enforces laws in a society.

Use Government in a sentence: Doesn't Jan understand that we are too busy dealing with our own lives to care what law the people running our government are or are not passing?

Political: Of, pertaining to, or concerned with politics.

Use Political in a sentence: They were very 'into' the conversation, but we just aren't political.

Political Party: A group of people wanting to take hold of power or influence government policy, usually by nominating their own candidates and trying to seat them in political office. There are typically 2 political parties in the United States, the Republicans and the Democrats.

Use Political Party in a sentence: It was bad enough that the spaghetti was dry and the pizza was cold, but once Jan and her boyfriend started asking us what political party we supported, it was time to go home.

The most powerful political parties in the United States are currently the Republican Party (Republicans) and the Democratic

Party (Democrats). There are others and now, more than ever, some are beginning to gain a larger following. Below are definitions of the most popular parties:

Republican: An advocate of a limited role of the Federal Government in solving the problems of society. The elephant represents this group. They are also referred to as the G.O.P. (Grand Old Party) and are generally considered to be 'conservative' or 'right-wing.'

Democrat: An advocate of democracy (a government by the people), believing in the political or social equality of all people. They are generally considered to be 'liberal' or 'left-wing.' The Donkey represents this group.

Independent: Not affiliated to any formal political party or ideology.

Libertarian: Believe that liberty is the core political value of modern civilization itself, the one that gives substance and form to all the other values of social life. Justice, prosperity, responsibility, tolerance, cooperation, and peace.

Green: A political party whose policies are based on concern for the environment.

Tea Party Movement: It endorses reduced government spending, opposition to taxation in varying degrees, reduction of the national debt and federal budget deficit, and adherence to an 'originalist' interpretation of the United States Constitution, but is not a recognized party.

Occupy Wall Street Movement: This movement highlights the growing gap between the rich and the poor, as currently large companies like those on Wall Street are making a lot of money while millions of Americans struggle to put food on the table. The focus seems to be to give more job opportunities to average Americans and to share in companies' prosperity. This is not a not a recognized party.

Interesting Fun Fact: Even though we've had republicans and democrats running the show for a very long time, the United States is NOT a two party system. You won't find anything in the Constitution about political parties at all, because the framers were completely against having political parties in our wonderful country. Learning from our history with Britain, they thought parties created unnecessary and counterproductive divisions within a nation. The notion of judging candidates based on their merits and their stand on the issues was a better idea.

Parting Words

There is much more to know about everything here. These are the basics to help build a framework. If you are interested in learning more I recommend a book called *The House and Senate Explained – The People's Guide to Congress*, by Ellen Greenberg. It's filled with helpful descriptions as well as a definition of phrases and words we hear on the news when talking about the House and Senate. If you are looking for more information on the three branches then head to www.VoteSmart.org, scroll to the bottom, and under the heading EDUCATION, click on '**Government 101**.'

The History Sprint

In order to have a working knowledge of politics and government, a quick hit of American history to reference can be useful. Below is a list of highlights of America's history. So put on your running shoes, don that baseball cap, and check your pulse as we get ready to run track for the history sprint!

Let's Take a Lap Around American Wars

1756-1763: The French and Indian War (also called the 7 year war) – This was a big war fought in several countries, but it's important to us, because the English and the French were fighting over domination of the colonies in North America (that's us), the Caribbean, and India. The English won, but the debt from the war almost wiped out the English government. This is what escalated the tensions that lead to the Revolutionary War, because England decided to tax us to get out of debt.

1775-1784: The Revolutionary War – We won our independence from England.

1812-1814: The War of 1812 – Also referred to as the second war for independence. There were alleged British violations of American shipping rights going on. American soldiers unsuccessfully attacked Canada, and the British retaliated by burning down our White House (such tempers!). America won this war too. The Star-Spangled Banner was written during this war.

1846-1848: The Mexican War – A war between the U.S. and Mexico, resulting in a treaty where we paid Mexico $15,000,000 for Texas, California, Arizona, New Mexico, Nevada, Utah and part of Colorado.

1861-1865: The Civil War – We fought ourselves. It all started by Lincoln's election as president. It was made worse by the slavery issues, and then had LOTS to do with deeply-rooted political and economic "stuff." The North and the South fought. The North won and ended the confederacy and slavery.

April 25, 1898–August 12, 1898: The Spanish-American War – The war between the US and Spain resulting in Spain's withdrawal from Cuba and its cession of Guam, the Philippines, and Puerto Rico.

1914–1918: World War I – A war between the allies (Russia, France, British Empire, Italy, United States, Japan, Romania, Serbia, Belgium, Greece, Portugal, Montenegro) and the Central Powers (Germany, Austria-Hungary, Turkey, Bulgaria). On April 6, 1917 – We formally declared war against Germany and won. The war officially ended the 11th hour of the 11th day of the 11th month of 1918.

1939-1945: World War II – Okay, pay attention, 'cuz this one reads like a soap opera!

The Allies (principally Britain, the Soviet Union, and the U.S.) defeated the Axis powers (principally Germany, Italy, and Japan). Britain and France declared war on Germany (Sept. 3, 1939) as a result of the German invasion of Poland (Sept. 1, 1939). Italy entered the war on June 10, 1940, shortly before the collapse of France (armistice signed June 22, 1940). On June 22, 1941, Germany attacked the Soviet Union, and on Dec. 7, 1941, the Japanese attacked the U.S. at Pearl Harbor, sooooo… , on December 8th, we declared war against Japan. On Sept. 8, 1943, Italy surrendered. The war in Europe ended on May 7, 1945 with the unconditional surrender of the Germans. The Japanese surrendered on August 14, 1945, as a direct result of the atomic bombs dropped by the Americans on Hiroshima and Nagasaki (cities in Japan).

1950-1953: Korean War – The war between South Korea, supported by the United Nations, and North Korea, supported by the People's Republic of China, with military material aid from the Soviet Union. A ceasefire stopped the fighting on July 27, 1953.

1955-1975: Vietnam War – The Vietnam War was a Cold War-era military conflict that occurred in Vietnam, Laos, and Cambodia from November 1955 to the fall of Saigon on April 30, 1975. This war followed the First Indochina War and was fought between North Vietnam, supported by its communist allies, and the government of South Vietnam, supported by the United States and other anti-communist nations. The U.S. part in the war ended in January of 1973 – Yes, we lost.

August 2, 1990–February 28, 1991: The Persian Gulf War – Commonly referred to as simply the Gulf War, was a war waged by a U.N.-authorized coalition force from thirty-four nations led by the United States, against Iraq in response to Iraq's invasion and annexation of the State of Kuwait.

September 20, 2001: The War On Terror – (Official name is: Overseas Contingency Operation or OCO) – Specifically refers to the ongoing military campaign led by the United States, United Kingdom, and their allies against organizations and regimes identified by them as terrorist, and excludes other independent counter-terrorist operations and campaigns such as those by Russia and India.

October 7, 2001 – May, 2014: The War in Afghanistan - The United States invaded the country after the September 11 attacks. Combat operations ended in 2014 and a small residual force remains there until the end of 2016.

March 20, 2003 – December 31, 2011: The War In Iraq - The Iraq War was an extended armed fight that began with the 2003 invasion of Iraq led by the United States. The government of Saddam Hussein collapsed as a result.

PRESIDENTS

You're on a hot streak! Feel the burn. Now drop and give me 44... presidents that is.

President	*Vice President*
1. George Washington (1789-1797)	John Adams (1789-1797)
2. John Adams (1797-1801)	Thomas Jefferson (1797-1801)

3. Thomas Jefferson (1801-1809) Aaron Burr (1801-1805)

 George Clinton (1805-1809)

4. James Madison (1809-1817) George Clinton (1809-1812)

 none (1812-1813)

 Elbridge Gerry (1813-1814)

 none (1814-1817)

5. James Monroe (1817-1825) Daniel D. Tompkins (1817-1825)

6. John Quincy Adams (1825-1829) John C. Calhoun (1825-1829)

7. Andrew Jackson (1829-1837) John C. Calhoun (1829-1832)

 none (1832-1833)

 Martin Van Buren (1833-1837)

8. Martin Van Buren (1837-1841) Richard M. Johnson (1837-1841)

9. William Henry Harrison (1841) John Tyler (1841)

10. John Tyler (1841-1845) none (1841-1845)

11. James K. Polk (1845-1849) George M. Dallas (1845-1849)

12. Zachary Taylor (1849-1850) Millard Fillmore (1849-1850)

13. Millard Fillmore (1850-1853) none (1850-1853)

14. Franklin Pierce (1853-1857) William King (1853)

 none (1853-1857)

15. James Buchanan (1857-1861) John C. Breckinridge (1857-1861)

16. Abraham Lincoln (1861-1865)

    Hannibal Hamlin (1861-1865)

    Andrew Johnson (1865)

17. Andrew Johnson (1865-1869)

    none (1865-1869)

18. Ulysses S. Grant (1869-1877)

    Schuyler Colfax (1869-1873)

    Henry Wilson (1873-1875)

    none (1875-1877)

19. Rutherford B. Hayes (1877-1881)

    William Wheeler (1877-1881)

20. James A. Garfield (1881)

    Chester Arthur (1881)

21. Chester Arthur (1881-1885)

    none (1881-1885)

22. Grover Cleveland (1885-1889)

    Thomas Hendricks (1885)

    none (1885-1889)

23. Benjamin Harrison (1889-1893)

    Levi P. Morton (1889-1893)

24. Grover Cleveland (1893-1897)

    Adlai E. Stevenson (1893-1897)

25. William McKinley (1897-1901)

    Garret Hobart (1897-1899)

    none (1899-1901)

    Theodore Roosevelt (1901)

26. Theodore Roosevelt (1901-1909)

    none (1901-1905)

    Charles Fairbanks (1905-1909)

27. William Howard Taft (1909-1913)

    James S. Sherman (1909-1912)

    none (1912-1913)

28. Woodrow Wilson (1913-1921)

    Thomas R. Marshall (1913-1921)

29. Warren G. Harding (1921-1923)	Calvin Coolidge (1921-1923)
30. Calvin Coolidge (1923-1929)	none (1923-1925)
	Charles Dawes (1925-1929)
31. Herbert Hoover (1929-1933)	Charles Curtis (1929-1933)
32. Franklin D. Roosevelt (1933-1945)	John Nance Garner (1933-1941)
	Henry A. Wallace (1941-1945)
	Harry S Truman (1945)
33. Harry S Truman (1945-1953)	none (1945-1949)
	Alben Barkley (1949-1953)
34. Dwight D. Eisenhower (1953-1961)	Richard Nixon (1953-1961)
35. John F. Kennedy (1961-1963)	Lyndon B. Johnson (1961-1963)
36. Lyndon B. Johnson (1963-1969)	none (1963-1965)
	Hubert Humphrey (1965-1969)
37. Richard Nixon (1969-1974)	Spiro Agnew (1969-1973)
	none (1973)
	Gerald Ford (1973-1974)
38. Gerald Ford (1974-1977)	none (1974)
	Nelson Rockefeller (1974-1977)
39. Jimmy Carter (1977-1981)	Walter Mondale (1977-1981)
40. Ronald Reagan (1981-1989)	George Bush (1981-1989)
41. George Bush (1989-1993)	Dan Quayle (1989-1993)

42. Bill Clinton (1993-2001)   Al Gore (1993-2001)

43. George W. Bush (2001-2009)   Dick Cheney (2001-2009)

44. Barack Obama (2009-present)   Joe Biden (2009-present)

We're in the final lap... don't pull a hammy! Here come the highlights of everything else that America has been a part of:

1776	Declaration of Independence arrives – We're gonna be free!
1784	Ben Franklin invents bifocal eyeglasses – We can SEE again!
1786	First ice cream made commercially in NYC – Rocky Road, please!
1787	Constitutional Convention – We have our own government!
1789	Bill of Rights adopted
1792	First U.S. Trade Union of shoemakers
1793	Fugitive Slave Act
1793	Eli Whitney invents cotton gin; revives dying slave economy of South
1798	Alien and Sedition Act
1808	Congress prohibits importing of African slaves
1814	The Invention of the power loom creates a factory occupation of weaving
1821	Missouri Compromise

1823	Monroe Doctrine
1829	Jackson introduces spoils system
1842	10-hour day for children under 12 in Massachusetts – Hope they offered a 401K!
1848	Gold discovered in California – It's money, it's a conductor... it's jewelry!
1854	Upper half of Indian Territory becomes part of Kansas Territory
1854	Republican Party formed for abolition of slavery
1854	Smith & Wesson invent revolver
1857	Dred Scott decision
1863	President Lincoln put out the Emancipation Proclamation, freeing slaves
1865	President Lincoln assassinated
1866	National Labor Union formed: first national association of unions
1868	8-hour day for federal employees
1865-77	Reconstruction in old South
1876	Sioux and Cheyenne defeat Custer at Little Big Horn, Montana
1876	National League founded (baseball)
1876	Alexander Graham Bell patents the telephone – The teenager was born!
1879	Thomas Edison invents incandescent light – Let there be light... all night long

1879	Female lawyers allowed to argue cases before Supreme Court
1883	Civil Service established
1886	Haymarket Square labor riot in Chicago kills eleven people
1887	Dawes Severality Act creates allotment system
1890	AFL founded by S Gompers (American Federation of Labor)
1890	Sherman Antitrust Act – 'You can 'play' Monopoly, but you cannot 'have' one.'
1892	Strike at Carnegie Steel results in ten deaths
1895	Wilhelm Rontgen discovers x-rays
1896	Supreme Court rules "separate but equal" legal
1901	President McKinley shot by anarchist
1902	President Theodore Roosevelt begins conservation of forests
1903	Wright Brothers fly first airplane
1904	President Theodore Roosevelt asserts U.S. right to intervene in Latin America
1907	Indian Territory becomes eastern half of Oklahoma
1908	GE patents electric toaster – Toast – YUM!
1909	NAACP in NYC
1909	20,000 female shirt makers in New York strike against sweatshop conditions

1914	August 3, World War One begins: Germany invades Belgium
1917	Russian revolutions: communist U.S.S.R. formed
1917	African Americans migrate north and west
1919	League of Nations created
1919	Iraq founded
1920	18th Amendment prohibits alcohol – Bummer.
1920	19th Amendment gives women right to vote
1927	Charles Lindbergh (Lucky Lindy) was the first person to fly the across the Atlantic Ocean non-stop
1929	Stock Market crashes and a worldwide depression begins
1933	Bureau of Indian Affairs reformed; sales of Indian lands halted
1933	Franklin Delano Roosevelt (FDR) starts the "New Deal"
1933	Prohibition repealed by the 21st amendment – Beer is legal again!
1934	Adolf Hitler becomes Fuehrer of Germany
1935	Social Security enacted to provide retirement insurance
1937	Dow Chemical develops plastics
1938	Fair Labor Standards Act establishes first minimum wage & 40-hour work week

1941	December 7 – Japan's surprise attack on Pearl Harbor
1943	All-American Girls Professional Baseball League founded
1945	United Nations formed
1945	U.S.A. bombs Japan
1947	Marshall Plan – U.S. was the only large power not significantly damaged by World War II. George Marshall created a plan to primarily rebuild the economy (and the spirit) of Western Europe.
1947	British India becomes Pakistan & India
1948	Israel founded
1948	NATO formed (North Atlantic Treaty Organization)'
1948 54	"McCarthyism" and the Second Red Scare transpired
1949	Child labor prohibited in Fair Labor Standards Act
1955	African Americans boycott buses in Montgomery, Alabama opposing racial segregation on public transit system
1955	Supreme Court orders school desegregation
1957	Soviets launch Sputnik, first artificial satellite
1961	President Kennedy created the Peace Corps
1961	First ICBM (Intercontinental Ballistic Missile – with a range greater than 5500 km.)

1961-69	Kennedy's Apollo project to land a man on the moon – Sadly, it was not made out of cheese
1960-65	Civil Rights movement
1962	Cuban missile crisis – A confrontation among the Soviet Union, Cuba and the United States in October, 1962
1963	Equal Pay Act establishes equal pay for women and men
1963	President Kennedy is assassinated
1964	Civil Rights Act restores tribal law to reservations
1965-70	Demonstrations against Vietnam War
1966-69	Hippie movement
1969	USA landed the first spacecraft on the Moon – "One small step for Man, One Giant Leap for Mankind!"
1970	EPA is created to enforce the Clean Air Act
1971	Soviet Salyut 1 space station
1971	Occupational Safety and Health Act
1973	Endangered Species Act
1973	Roe v. Wade
1973-74	President Nixon resigns due to the Watergate scandal – He swears he was "not a crook."
1970s	Industry begins shifting production to low-wage countries
1976	Viking 1 & 2 land on Mars

The History Sprint

1978	Personal computer appears
1980s	CD, VCR, & cable are everyday items
1980-2000	AFSCME (government workers) and SEIU (sanitation workers) grow
1983	Reagan increases military funding after proposing Star Wars (space-based anti-missile system)
1980s	"War on Drugs" jails 1/5 of young black men. Prison populations doubled... and the international narcotics trade continued to thrive.
1987	Ozone "hole" found over Antartica
1987	Gorbachev (leader of the Soviet Union) tears down the Berlin Wall (a symbol of communism)
1989-91	U.S.S.R dissolves into republics; Cold War over
1993	Family and Medical Leave Act
1993	The World Wide Web says HELLO!
1996	Welfare reform
1997	Robust economy creates longest prosperity in U.S. history
1997	NASA spacecraft lands on Mars
1998	International Space Station begins construction
1999	Budget goes into surplus
2000s	Animals are cloned – Oh, if only I'd kept a strand of fur!
2000s	Increasing development of solar energy sources
2000s	China emerges as economic giant

2001	9/11 Terrorist Attack
2008-09	Global financial crisis and recession
2008	The first African American wins the Presidency
2011	Occupy Wall Street Begins
2009-10	The 'Tea Party' emerges
2011	Osama bin Laden killed by Seal Team Six – America takes its first deep breath since 9/11.
2013	Federal Government "Shuts Down" for 16 days
2014	ACA (Affordable Care Act) goes into effect – Pre-existing conditions no longer exist
2015	Supreme Court declares same-sex marriage legal in all 50 states

Parting Words

You did it! Grab a snack and be sure to hydrate! This is a quick hit guide to provide a basic framework. If your interest was stirred by something in particular, there are many books and documentaries on every subject. Check out your local library for more information, and **www.freedocumentaries.org** is a great website on which to watch free documentaries.

That was some great cardio! Next up – Toning!

Get Out That Yoga Mat!

Time to sculpt and shape your body...
of Opinions

Politicians ought to have an ideology; a body of opinions. The reason for this is because many or most of the decisions that an elected official must make on our behalf are not known before an election. If we are going to vote for that person then we must use another way to measure ability. Their ideology functions like a promise to us. We can judge the politician seeking our vote by his/her politics and character. We decide whether or not we share the candidate's political principles, and if we believe that person holds true to them when new issues come up. Being able to do this requires that we hold their ideology and body of opinions up to our own. This is where many people stop because we don't think we have a body of opinions to compare to. We absolutely do.

Ideology: A framework of basic principles; a set of ideals that constitute one's goals, expectations, and actions. It can be thought of as a comprehensive vision, a way of looking at things.

We all hold them. We just may not have thought them through, written them out, or formally declared them to ourselves. When you don't hold a personal body of opinions then you can fall under attack by the media, politicians and political pundits as they work to make THEIR opinions YOUR opinions. Once you develop them for yourself, you will feel the freedom of no longer being affected by the constant pettiness of those trying to push their views on you. You can pick and choose what you want to make a part of your body of opinions, and you can more easily reject things you want to disagree with because you will know why you feel the way you feel.

Building a Body

Partisanship is at its best when it is about ideology. Ideology is not blind loyalty or refusal to evaluate new evidence. It's a framework of your basic principles and values. To uncover some of yours all you have to do is go through the list below and spend a few days paying attention to your thoughts on those topics. When you have time or when you feel like it, grab a notebook and write down your thoughts on them.

Partisanship: Showing favoritism to one's own party.

ISSUES:

- Campaign Financing
- Civil Rights
- Defense
- Disabilities
- Economy
- Education
- Energy & Environment
- Environment
- Ethics
- Foreign Policy
- Global Threats and National Security
- Health Care
- Homeland Security
- Immigration
- Minimum Wage
- Retirement
- Seniors & Social Security
- Strengthening Family Life
- Taxes
- Technology
- Urban Policy
- Veterans
- Women

Write down any of the above topics that speak to you and write a stream of consciousness about each of them. See what you feel on a gut level and then go from there in building fact under feeling. And, if you change your mind along the way based on what you learn, then so be it. Make sure your opinions can stand up to scrutiny. Someone should be able to ask you more than one or two questions before you have trouble talking about it knowledgeably. A framework is not just a list of opinions. All the pieces should come together to become your personal ideology and body of opinions.

Get Out That Yoga Mat

Here are some questions you can ask yourself along the way:

- How do I feel about this issue?

- What do I know, or think I know, about this issue?

- Is this my opinion or the opinion of someone else that I've taken on (such as a parent, spouse, friend or significant other)?

- Have I looked at this situation from all angles?

- Have I listened to my emotional instinct? (If it feels good then you are done. If it feels uncertain then think it out again.)

- Is this choice good for me and/or for my family? (Listen to what your heart says here)

- Have I done research on different sides of this topic? If I have, did I make a snap decision, or did I consider all of the evidence I came across, not just the stuff I liked?

- Do I need to consult a friend or acquaintance who has experience on this topic?

- Have I been rational and reasoned in my decision?

- Am I comfortable in my decision on this topic?

Another easy way to recognize values you hold is when you feel someone has trampled on them. If you find yourself feeling hurt or offended by something a person said or did, think it through to the full conclusion of why you feel that way. The 'why' is actually your opinion on the subject. If you hear a thought or opinion that feels wrong to you, define the wrong. If you read something and you disagree with the author's point of view, try to pinpoint what exactly you disagree with. When someone speaks and you find yourself nodding along, search your mind for the 'big picture' behind your approval. These things will help you define principles and values that you hold. As you fit all of these pieces together you will have created a framework on which to build. That framework becomes your personal body of opinions.

If you want politicians and elected officials to speak to your issues make sure you know what they are.

If you find you have strong opinions on an issue, but have no facts or valid reasons to support it don't throw away your opinion. Instead, look into it. People exist who don't agree with you, and that's okay. Occasionally try to read, watch or listen to people who disagree with you. Become more informed and you may find the information you are looking for to either support or shift how you feel. Either way, you will be in a position to enrich your body of opinions. The rule of thumb is, though you never need enter into a debate, be prepared to defend or debate your position so you know you've thought out your ideas well.

While a general knowledge of the most important topics can be invaluable, learn about what speaks to you and ignore the rest. If you don't care about the topic then choose to go to your child's little league game instead of crosschecking facts on the validity of President Obama's birth certificate. If it's been a long day, decide to veg in front of the TV instead of boning up on Immigration Policy.

Thoughtful Reflection

Good answers to complex problems deserve consideration and thoughtful reflection, so take your time with the ones that matter to you.

Parting words

Having an ideology shows you have thought things through, but it is not a substitute for thinking. You can use your body of opinions now and then during the debates to make political decisions for yourself. Lastly, having them doesn't mean sharing them. Unless you want to, you don't have to discuss your personal body of opinions with anyone. They are yours.

Thoughts become words
Words become actions
Actions become character
And character is everything

Avoid the Media: Think for Yourself

In Search of the Justice League:

"Faster than a WIFI connection! More powerful than a high def Flat Screen! Enabling Americans to spread tall tales in a single round of conversation!"

"Look! Up in the sky!"

"It's a bird!"

"It's a plane!"

No, it's the heinous Super Villain… "They Say!"

"They say" an apple a day keeps the doctor away.

"They say" people are living longer than ever before.

"They say" Chris Christie is a RINO.

"They say" Obama is Anti-American.

RINO: Republicans whose political views or actions are considered insufficiently conservative. Republican In Name Only.

Do not trust this super villain. *"They say"* is enticing, but do not be misled! The dastardly *"They Say"* is a criminal among criminals and seeks to destroy the very fabric of our country! We must band together as Americans and fight. It will be difficult. "They Say" is powerful and grows stronger each time someone utters its name. "They say people are having fewer babies since the recession." "They say the housing market is improving." "They say Americans are disappointed the president didn't follow through on his promises." *"They say* Bush doesn't understand problems faced by ordinary Americans."

49

Every time these unconfirmed statements are repeated in "They Say's" name its power grows and our nation weakens. Rest assured the one and only antidote has been discovered. We can defeat this treacherous villain and make communication safe again.

Slaying the Super Villain: It is as simple as answering one little question: Who is 'They?' If you can't answer that question then, Game Over. Return your lips to their full, upright and locked position. If you are spreading information that you have not verified, and you did so by using the evil "They Say," then you have aided and abetted this elusive villain, and accidentally made yourself part of the problem. The problem being that if we don't know what we are talking about, we are not communicating, we are gossiping.

When someone is telling you something that requires them to say, "I heard," "they say," "It was reported that," "studies show" or some version of that, beware. The next time someone says something like this to you, try asking them where he/she heard it and who 'they' is. Be respectful. No need to tear someone down when you can politely seek the truth. You will be astounded at how quickly even the wisest people in your circle may crumble as they realize they can't support their words. The next time you catch yourself doing it, ask yourself the same question. There is no shame in not knowing something, but recklessly passing off half-heard truths or made up gossip as fact is wrong. It is especially wrong if someone else will be paying the price for our wagging tongues.

If someone can validate their words it is next your duty to apply your own logic to the statement to decide if it rings true to you. Let's take apart an old *"They say"* statement:

First, let me tell you a little about Al Gore. Al Gore is a Democrat who ran for president in 2000 against Republican George W. Bush. That election had serious problems in Florida and was so hotly debated it not only went to the Florida Supreme Court, but America went without a winner for 36 days until finally the presidency was awarded to George W. Bush. Al Gore moved on and began educating the public about global warming with a comprehensive slide show he put together that, in 2006, was turned into a world famous documentary called An Inconvenient Truth. This documentary won many awards, Al Gore won the Nobel Peace Prize and the film made $49 million dollars. There were people who loved it and people who hated it. There were people who felt that global warming was a myth and people who felt their eyes had been opened to its effects. There were those who thought Al Gore was amazing and those who thought he was a sour grapes hypocrite.

Now that you have the background, here is the "They Say" statement: "They say Gore made all that up about the environment. Did you know he spends $3,000 a month on his electric bill?"

This statement made national news at the time. It seemed designed to attack Al Gore and his credibility. To deactivate this "They say" we would start with where you might have heard this. If it was spoken second hand then it would be important to ask where that person came by this information. Did he/she hear it on a bus, the radio, TV, in a coffee shop? If it can be traced back to those who consider themselves to be a credible source, AKA members of the media, the next set of questions must come into play: Where did that outlet get that information from? Who verified its validity? Was this statement taken out of context? Is that dollar amount accurate and what exactly constitutes Former Vice President Al Gore's 'electric bill?' Does that negate the validity of a documentary that outlined global warming? Is this statement relevant to the information provided in his documentary? Should this "They say" shape our thoughts on the environment?

I don't know where it started, but media outlets repeated the statement in various ways. What was this statement designed to illicit from us and whose agenda was being served when the statement was put out into the media? Does the member of the media who said it have something to gain by making the statement? Is the statement Fair and Accurate? If it is, is it the whole truth? Who says so and how credible do you find this person and why? It may seem like a lot of work, but it only takes minutes. That doesn't seem like much time, compared to mindlessly accepting and spreading gossip that could actually destroy a person's career or life's work. Seek the source, consider the source, then decide if you find the source and the information credible.

Let's remember this country is made up of 300 million individual people. When someone is being attacked, give him or her the courtesy of getting the whole story before spreading incorrect, possibly hurtful, information. It's not an exact science. There are times when we are absolutely lied to, even when great reporters have dug for the truth. It does happen, but what happens so much more often is misrepresentation by those tending to personal agendas, and we have absolute power over that. When we hear "Studies show"… "A new report suggests"… "Doctors claim," all we have to do is ask the next few questions. Who did the study? What was the focus of the report? Who paid for it? Was the doctor paid for his or her opinion on this topic? The more we challenge the people who make up *the media* the more they will find themselves compelled to tell the truth and to be FAIR in order to avoid our scrutiny.

And since we must do first by example, we have to hold ourselves to the same standards. Before repeating something or spreading a rumor, check the facts. On important world issues such as choosing a president and running the government, it is downright dangerous to decide to accept or pass on rumor as fact. Below is an example of what happens when this important step is ignored:

Many people have had this email forwarded to them or heard about its contents from a co-worker or friend:

You Starbucks fans read this. Starbucks view on the war Dear everyone:
Please pass this along to anyone you know, this needs to get out in the open.

Recently Marines over in Iraq supporting this country in OIF wrote to Starbucks because they wanted to let them know how much they liked their coffee and try to score some free coffee grounds.

Starbucks wrote back telling the Marines thanks for their support in their business, but that they don't support the War and anyone in it and that they won't send them the Coffee.

So as not to offend them we should not support in buying any Starbucks products.

As a War vet and writing to you patriots I feel we should get this out in the open. I know this War might not be very popular with some folks, but that doesn't mean we don't support the boys on the ground fighting street to street and house to house for what they and I believe is right.

If you feel the same as I do then pass this along, or you can discard it and I'll never know.

Thanks very much for your support to me, and I know you'll all be there again here soon when I deploy once more.

It's very compelling, right? It's also untrue. This misinformation was spread by those willing to believe what was put before them and worse, willing to forward on this unsubstantiated information as fact. Since 2004 millions of people have shown their solidarity against an injustice that never existed. When I received this email I decided to verify the information. I picked up the phone and called the Starbucks customer service number. The man on the line was more than happy to explain this unfortunate situation and then provided me with the Sergeant's follow up email:

Dear Readers,

Almost 5 months ago I sent an e-mail to you my faithful friends. I did a wrong thing that needs to be cleared up. I heard by word of mouth about how Starbucks said they didn't support the war and all. I was having enough of that kind of talk and didn't do my research properly like I should have. This is not true. Starbucks supports men and women in uniform. They have personally contacted me and I have been sent many copies of their company's policy on this issue. So I apologize for this quick and wrong letter that I sent out to you.

*Now I ask that you all pass this email around to everyone you
passed the last one to.
Thank you very much for understanding about this.*

We have control in these situations. We simply have to choose to
take that control. I decided to hit 'reply all' on the forward and
send a copy of the retracted email. I encouraged them to call Starbucks themselves to confirm it, and to clear this matter up with
anyone they may have sent the first email to. Fact checking was
new for this group. Instead of a thank you, I was removed from
the forward list, destined to never receive another chain letter.
Brutal punishment.

Hey! I'm a Busy Person and I Don't Care

That's fine. You don't have to get involved at all. When a "They
Say" enters your space you always have three choices:

1. Blindly share information as fact to everyone you know
    (Puh-leeze don't pick this one)

2. Ignore something you have heard and move on

3. Investigate and respond

Decide which one works best for you and then commit to it. Easy-
Peasy.

Now that you see how you can check yourself, let's move on to the
biggest "They Say" culprits out there: **The Media**

The media is not a 'machine;' it's a label put on a large group of
people with access to cameras and money. Many of them may be
jaded and greedy, but they are people. Corporate decisions are
NOT *'not personal.'* They are very personal to the financial bottom line of the company *rainmakers*. The meetings in the news-
rooms to see what 'news' gets cut and what makes it to us is
largely based on keeping the viewer's attention and their sponsors
happy. And when you see segments on Hollywood celebrities being put up as hard news next to military coverage where many

of our friends and family members are serving, you can clearly see where the media puts its focus. It's a competitive market to be sure, and that's why we have to be aware of its severe limitations.

Rainmaker: A person who is highly financially successful, especially in business.

The people who make up the media believe they control us because we are unlikely to stop and weigh and balance what they choose to serve up to us. These are lyrics from a popular John Mayer song: "And when you trust your television what you get is what you got. 'Cause when they own the information oh, they can bend it all they want." Well, admittedly we humans have a tendency to latch on to small bits of unconfirmed information and then make large assumptions based on facts that weren't provided.

Advertisers and media owners choose what to show us based on what makes them look good or keeps them from looking bad. Any goings-on that they don't want you to know about is highly unlikely to be seen, heard or reported on – which is not to say we didn't need to know about it. If you'd like some humorous insight on this topic, I direct you to **Conspiracy Theory Rock** found on Youtube. It's a short video done in the School House Rock fashion, but clearly a satiric adult exploration of how American media functions. Go to **www.Youtube.com** and type into the search box **Conspiracy Theory Rock**. It is the Mediaopoly cartoon video.

ABC, CBS, NBC, WGN, CNN, CNBC, CSPAN, MSNBC, FOX

It's not our job to keep them wealthy. We are not here to serve them. They are here to serve us, but no matter how many times CNN says they are the most trusted name in news, they, like every other news outlet (and network and cable station, and newspaper and...) are bound by their advertisers. They exist to make money, because they are a business. Fairness and accuracy in reporting (FAIR) may be very important but it pales in comparison to losing advertising dollars. Many pundits and TV reporters are there largely to grab headlines and make money. Some do it with pride, respect and well researched information. Some do it by simply conveying whatever information is given to them without questioning it, some passing off personal opinion as fact.

What this means is that if the people in the business of delivering news have placed making money as their number one goal, then we the viewers have a FAIR problem. We can't be getting fair and accurate information if the people providing that information don't answer to us. We have the power to do two things about this:

1. Use your own good judgment when you see or hear something that sounds suspicious. Our personal judgment is subject only to us. And if you are a news watcher, keep an ear out for how many times in a month your station of choice makes a 'correction' or 're-reports' on something with a completely different focus. It happens frequently – they are just quiet about it. It is okay to say, "I don't believe what I heard on the news today."

2. Disallow misbehavior from the media. We have the power to question the media or even the FCC (Federal Communications Commission) itself. The more we call the media on misinformation, half truths and straight up gossip the more their credibility will erode, which affects viewers. Viewers = Sponsors. Sponsors = Money. And what is making money? Their number one goal. They. Are. A. Business. And we have far more power than we realize.

Don't you DARE tell me to 'Write a Letter!'

Compelling good behavior by the media is even more important in an election year. Our job is to choose the next president. We deserve to have the most FAIR and balanced information members of the media can give us. We all know what an annoyance it is to have somebody tell us the importance of getting involved. If you don't like something you are supposed to make a phone call or write a letter. "Write your congressman." "Call your representative." "Drop a line to your local paper." "Tell the media what's on your mind." Why is it nobody ever tells us HOW to do these things? And don't you love how they don't help you with things like addresses, phone numbers or an email?? Well, let's fix that. At the end of this chapter is a short section on how to write a letter to an elected official or to a member of the media. Following that will be a contact list of major media outlets (TV, Radio, Newspaper, Magazine), the address for the President, as well as instructions on getting the name and address for your U.S. Representative and U.S. Senator.

Federal Communications Commission (FCC): An independent government agency that regulates interstate and international communications by radio, television, wire, cable, and satellite.

When you want to complain to the advertisers, you can find the corporate address by searching online for the corporate office, or going to your local library and asking the research librarian to help you locate the corporate address and the CEO, President or Public Relations Department of that company. One of those three should receive your letter. Email is often preferable, but sending a written letter seems to hold more weight with people. You decide.

By giving the power back to the people it will stop being about advertisers selling us products and start being about doing better work. So, make a phone call, send an email, letter, fax, carrier pigeon or owl to express your concern. If you don't see the address you are looking for, virtually all media addresses are available in the **Gale Directory of Publications and Broadcast Media**, which you can find at the library. If you are willing to search around a little on the internet you can usually find a contact person and address for just about any company or organization.

The most important part of controlling the media has to do with respecting one another. Though a person may be wealthy, famous, or in the public eye, they are still a person and deserve fairness. Whisper campaigns, smear campaigns, muck raking... Get the facts. Get them from the horse's mouth... and then question the horse. Be a gatekeeper to honesty and it will serve us all well.

Media Medics

Have you ever been bitten by something? A cat, a dog, a spider, a snake? Well, I am here to tell you that there is no bite more deadly or unforgiving than the dreaded and unpredictable sound bite. The effects are immediate and people live and die by how quickly the bite is treated or if it is allowed to spread. Sound bites are designed to lift someone up without proper cause or smash them to the ground in the same fashion. The sound bite seeks to grab your attention and focus it on a microscopic phrase in someone's sentence. It pulls the words viciously out of context and repeats them over and over again until the listeners find themselves falling away from their own thoughts, brainwashed and delirious. Sound bites can strike at any time and their very existence is a breeding ground for spin.

Sound Bite: A brief, striking remark or statement excerpted from an audiotape or videotape for insertion in a broadcast news story. A short extract from a recorded interview, chosen for its pungency or appropriateness.

Spin: To provide an interpretation of a statement or event, especially in a way meant to sway public opinion.

The sound bite can kill you in the media. A lifetime of credible, honest living can be washed away in the blink of an eye by repeated attacks from just one fatal sound bite. Here is an example:

On August 19, 2012, Republican Congressman Todd Akin made a gaffe during a TV interview on The Jaco Report. He is strongly pro-life, and during an almost 20 minute interview covering many different topics, he was asked whether abortion should be allowed in the case of rape. Among the other things said, his response was that it was his understanding from doctors that it's rare for someone to become pregnant from rape. He said, "If it's a legitimate rape, the female body has ways to try to shut that whole thing down." He went on to say: "But let's assume that maybe that didn't work or something. I think there should be some punishment, but the punishment ought to be on the rapist and not attacking the child." It was an amicable interview and their discussion went on and then came to a pleasant end.

Gaffe: An unintentional remark causing embarrassment to its originator; a blunder.

Unfortunately, Congressman Akin was running for U.S. Senator and this sound bite immediately made national headlines. People were taking issue with the word 'legitimate' and his notion that a woman's body can 'shut down a pregnancy' when raped. The Democrats circulated his comment citing statistics regarding rape and pregnancy. The congressman was then asked to step out of the race for Senator by Republican presidential hopeful Mitt Romney. The Republican Party itself asked him to step out of the race, all because of a gaffe. Nobody could hear him saying that he made a mistake, that he meant to say 'forcible' rape or that he spoke in error, as they were too busy putting his entire career on the line because of one sound bite.

The next day, Monday, August 20th, the congressman was invited to talk to Governor Mike Hukabee on the radio, where he made a human apology for the gaffe: "I made a couple of serious mistakes that were just wrong and I need to apologize for those. First, I might say that I have always been committed to pro-life, and it was because I didn't want to harm the most vulnerable. But likewise I care deeply for the victims who've been raped and they're equally vulnerable. And a rape is equally tragic. And I made that statement in error. Let me be clear: Rape is never legitimate. It's an evil act. It's committed by violent predators. I used the wrong words in the wrong way. What I said was ill conceived and it was wrong, and for that I apologize. I'm a dad of two daughters. I want tough justice for sexual predators. I've always had a compassionate heart for the victims of sexual assault. And I've even known some women who have been raped and I know that it is a terrible, terrible thing. That those consequences extend many, many, many years later. And I also know that people do become pregnant from rape, and I didn't mean to imply that that wasn't the case. It does happen. And it's also terrible, particularly the most terrible of all. And I really just want to apologize to those that I've hurt, because as I said I have spoken in error. I wanted to get that straight right off the bat."

Congressman Akin was favored to win before being infected by the sound bite, "legitimate Rape." As a result he lost the election. This was a deadly sound bite. But what can we do about it? How can we combat this ruthless virus? Is there any way to stop it? At last the antidote has been discovered. It is simple and it is powerful:

Check the facts. Read, listen to or watch the entire segment the sound bite was pulled from then come to your own conclusions. If you agree you can move on. If you do not, then you can take the next step by telling others what you learned. You can also contact the people or media outlet that 'bit' you and tell them how you feel about it. You can firmly request better behavior from those in your circle, and of the media you can request that the spin be reversed and the sound bite publicly destroyed.

When I heard the sound bite I decided to watch the entire interview. While it was true, he made a mistake in his words, the context made a very big difference to me. In my opinion, his character and manner did not match his words, and I saw that he'd been a pro-life U.S. Congressman since 2001. Like him or hate him, the Congressman already won a tough primary and had earned his name on the ballot. Believe him or don't, he stood up and admitted, with deep sincerity, he made a mistake. I did not write the media to complain, as this sound bite had exploded within hours and was widespread. I did opt to ignore the sound bite.

Again, it's simpler than it seems to control the media and how it affects us. Respect the person who was 'bitten' and commit to grasping the entirety of something before taking it as law. Now, if there is a sound bite looming over the public that you don't care about or don't want to invest the time in, that's okay. Simply disallow that information to impact your life. This means not adding it to your personal body of opinions, not giving it credibility when you hear it repeated by the media or by others in your circle. This also means not repeating it yourself.

Pundits: Professional reporters, political operatives or cheap hack entertainers?

When you are watching a recap of the day's news on a news station or on the radio, who are the people talking and rebutting? What is their credibility to interpret what we were presented by the news reporters? Why should *their spin* on the matter, matter at all? These pundits then bring on guest pundits to talk even more about what was just reported on. Why? We are more than able to make up our own minds for ourselves. Watch them if you are interested, but keep an open mind with these *spin* artists. Make certain you trust the people talking and understand why they have been selected. Are they hawking a book? Were they chosen by a political party to *spin* for them? What is his/her expertise on the topic at hand? Give their body of opinions only the weight you believe they deserve, and always weigh them much lighter than your own body of opinions.

Pundit: An expert in a particular subject or field who is frequently called on to give opinions about it to the public.

Canceling the Swimsuit competition. "Who put him in *that* shirt?" "Did the haircut really cost $400?" "What's the deal with the comb over?" "That candidate is way too short to be president." It's easy to lump all television together as entertainment. In many cases it's harmless, but in this situation we are electing a government official and the superficial shouldn't get in the way. How someone dresses isn't as important as what he or she says. It is also unimportant how they gestured or looked away from camera when they said it. There is an old saying, "Where you go and what you do tells people who you are." The media believe consumers want the kind of reporting that is personality over policy and style over substance. Show them they are wrong.

We are looking for someone who speaks to our issues and resonates with us. We have real problems that need solving. We don't have time to indulge the cosmetic ones. Know what your issues are and know where the candidates stand on them. The power is not in the *Power Tie*. The media will fuel a fire if they think it will generate some heat for their station. Someone on TV giving the superficial credibility does not mean it *has* credibility. This is a time for high-minded debate. Let's all remember to Avoid the Media and Think For Ourselves.

Parting words

If you want more on the subject of the media I refer you to **Choosing the President 2008: A Citizen's guide to the Electoral Process**, put out by the League of Women Voters. I also refer you to **Abandoned in the Wasteland: Children, Television, and the First Amendment** written by Newt Minnow, former Federal Communications Commission Chair. And if you feel supercharged to get involved with keeping the media in line, then I invite you to take a look at FAIR's Media Activist Kit. It's online and has "how-to" guides for identifying, documenting, and challenging inaccurate or unfair news coverage. There is also information on promoting independent media. Just go to **www.fair.org**, click on '**Take Action**,' then look under the photo and click on '**Media Activism Kit**'.

Great people talk about ideas, average people talk about things,
and small people talk about others.
Author Unknown

Choose to be Extraordinary.

The Pen IS Mightier Than the Sword!
(But I still wouldn't bring it to a sword fight)

Writing a letter is patriotic, it's responsible... it's SCARY! Not many of us rub elbows with the political set or members of the media. Writing a letter opens us up to an attack on our education level, our ideologies and even our grammar. It can feel worrisome, but this is one of those defining moments where we as Americans have to say, "So WHAT? You are *my* elected official, or you run the media *I* pay for and you work for me. Regardless of my faults I deserve to be heard."

It may feel like we are left out in the cold by our elected officials or with media outlets, but the truth is we have a lot of sway when enough of us let them know what's on our mind. And you don't have to talk about only complaints or wrongs you want to right. What about letting your elected official know who you are as a constituent? What about letting the media know the kind of information you want to know more about? They represent us. Tell them how many children you have, what kind of challenges you face, what you miss in your life that the government or the media could play a role in. What does a day in your life look like? Tell them about the kind of voter you are, and the kind of things you'll be looking for out of them during their term in office, or the kind of information you use from the media to make your decision on who to vote for.

Constituent: Person being represented by an elected official.

Keep It Simple

Your letter should address a single topic or issue. Ranting and rambling not only sends an unclear message, it increases the possibility that you will not be taken seriously.

If you want a response you must include your name and address, even if you are sending an email. Typed, one-page letters with no more than three paragraphs are the best, whether it's an email or paper letter. The three paragraphs should be structured like this:

1. Tell them who you are and explain why you are writing.

2. Give details. Remove as much emotion as you can and present them with facts. Be laser beam specific and honest about how the topic affects you and others. If you are writing about a certain bill, please cite the correct title or number of the bill if you can (more info on that shortly). Describe it well if you can't.

3. This last paragraph is where you should ask about the action you want taken. An example is that you want them to vote for or against a bill, consider a new law, change a policy, etc.

As a Side Note:

Even though snail mail letters are well received (everybody likes getting stuff in the mail) ever since anthrax was found in congressional buildings in 2001, mail to Congress can take about a month to be delivered. If your issue is a timely one, you might want to stick with an email.

SAMPLE LETTER

(Your Name Here)

123 Main Street

Somewhere, IL 54321

(Date)

The Honorable Dick Durbin

711 Hart Senate Building
Washington, DC 20510

Dear Senator Durbin,

I am disappointed that 100 men and women can't seem to put aside personal or 'party' differences to address the job loss in this country. I am the mother of three children and we are barely able to make ends meet. The electric company has been allowed to increase our cost by 20%, before taxes are added in, and my water bill has increased 30%. My husband's job has cut his hours and is looking at layoffs, because they are a small business. This government is not providing help for small businesses.

I wish you would have acted as quickly to this problem as you all acted with a bail out when the banking industry collapsed on itself in 2008. It seems that you are not acting at all. Please take the jobs bill **HR 89098** seriously and begin working on it instead of allowing it to be held up in red tape. It's wrong and it's hurting real people like me.

We need your help. Please find a way to begin working on jobs bill HR 89098. It's time to get back to work.

Respectfully,

Place your name here

Congress uses codes to describe what they are working on. If your letter refers to a piece of legislation put it in your letter.

House Bill: "**H.R.**_____" (Place bill number here)

House Simple Resolution: "**H.RES.**_____" (Place House Resolutions number here)

House Joint Resolution: "**H.J.RES.**_____" (Place House Joint Resolution number here)

Senate Bill: "**S.__**" (Place Senate Bills here)

Senate Simple Resolution: "**S.RES.**_____" (Place Senate Resolutions here)

Senate Joint Resolution: "**S.J.RES.**_____" (Place Senate Joint Resolutions here)

Bill: A written document that suggests a new law.

House Bill: A bill originating in the U.S. House of Representatives.

Senate Bill: A bill originating in the Senate.

Resolution: A firm decision to do or not to do something.

Simple Resolution: In the United States, a simple resolution is a legislative measure passed by only either the Senate or the House.

Joint Resolution: A resolution passed by both houses of Congress.

Addressing the President and Members of Congress

Rather than providing an email address, both Congressman and Senators require us to fill out a contact email form. You can go to your public library and ask them to give you the list of U.S. Congressmen and U.S. Senators in your state or you can go online and retrieve the info. Here's how:

Contact a U.S. Congressman:

Go to **www.house.gov** and click on '**Representatives.**' A Directory of Representatives will pop up and on the top right of the page you will be prompted to enter your zip code. When you do, the Congressman and his/her name and all district information will be provided. Click on the name to be brought to his/her home page. Their contact information is almost always right on top. They want to hear from us.

Beginning the letter:

Dear Congressman/Congresswoman:

Contact a U.S. Senator:

Go to **www.senate.gov** and click on '**Senators.**' A page will pop up with three choices: '**Choose a State,**' '**Choose a Senator,**' '**Choose a Class.**' You will go to '**Choose a State.**' Click on your state and your two U.S. Senators will pop up. Their phone numbers are on this page, and you can click on their web form to contact them via email. If you wish to send snail mail, then click on his/her name and be taken to the Senator's website. Click on **Contact** and the street addresses for all offices should be listed at the bottom of the email form.

Beginning the letter:

Dear Senator:

White House:

President Obama (or whomever you want to read your letter)

The White House
1600 Pennsylvania Avenue NW
Washington, DC 20500

Phone: 202-456-1414

Comments: 202-456-1111

Email – They require you to fill out an on-line contact form. Go to www.whitehouse.gov and click on **'Submit Questions and Comments'.**

Beginning the letter:

Dear Mr., Ms., Mrs. President (place full name here)

Media Contact Information

Some of these institutions do not provide an email, but rather an 'email form' accessed only on their websites. The easiest way to contact these companies electronically is by going to **www.fair.org.** Click on **'Take Action'** and then go to the bottom of that page titled Activism Resources. There you will find FAIR's **'Media Contact List.'** Click on that and the list of names and email form links will come up.

Beginning the letter:

To Whom It May Concern:

Network/Cable Television

ABC News - www.abcnews.go.com
47 West 66th Street, New York, NY 10023
Phone: 212-456-7777 / 212-456-7000
Email: form on website under 'contact us'

BBC Worldwide Americas - www.bbcamerica.com
747 3rd Avenue, New York, NY 10017.
Email: form on website under 'contact us'

CBS News - www.cbsnews.com
524 W. 57th St., New York, NY 10019
Phone: 212-975-4321

CBS Evening News: evening@cbsnews.com
Face the Nation: facethenation@cbsnews.com
60 Minutes: 60m@cbsnews.com

48 Hours: 48hours@cbsnews.com
Email: form on website under 'contact us'

CNBC - www.cnbc.com
900 Sylvan Avenue, Englewood Cliffs, NJ 07632
Phone: 201-735-2622
Email: info@cnbc.com

CNN - www.cnn.com
One CNN Center, Atlanta, GA 30303
Phone: 404-827-1500
Situation Room: situationroom@cnn.com
Email: form on website under 'contact us'

Fox News Channel - www.foxnews.com
1211 Avenue of the Americas, New York, NY 10036
Phone: 212-301-3000
comments@foxnews.com
Special Report With Bret Baier:special@foxnews.com

The O'Reilly Factor: oreilly@foxnews.com
Hannity: hannity@foxnews.com
Email: form on website under 'contact us'

MSNBC/NBC - www.MSNBC.com or www.NBCNEWS.com
30 Rockefeller Plaza, New York, NY 10112
Phone: 212-664-4444

Hardball: hardball@msnbc.com
Dateline NBC: dateline@nbcuni.com
NBC Nightly News: nightly@nbc.com
NBC News Today: today@nbc.com
Email: form on website under 'contact us'

PBS - www.pbs.org
2100 Crystal Drive, Arlington, VA 22202-3785
Phone: 703-739-5000
Phone: 703-739-5290 (Michael Getler)

PBS NewsHour: newsdesk@newshour.org

Frontline: frontline@pbs.org
Email: form on website under 'contact us'

National Radio Programs

National Public Radio - www.npr.org
1111 North Capitol Street, NE, Washington, DC 20002
Phone: 202-513-2000 / 202-513-3232
Email: form on website under 'contact us'

The Rush Limbaugh Show - www.rushlimbaugh.com
1270 Avenue of the Americas, New York, NY 10020
Phone: 800-282-2882 / 212-445-3900
Kit Carson, Producer: 212-445-3966
E-mail: rush@eibnet.com

Sean Hannity Show - www.hannity.com
Phone: 800-941-7326 (On-Air 3-6 p.m.)
Lynda McLaughlin, Producer: 212-896-5302
Email: lynda@hannity.com

POTUS – Politics of the United States, SiriusXM
P.O. Box 33174, Detroit, MI 48232
866-967-6887
Email: potus@siriusxm.com

National Newspapers

The Los Angeles Times - www.latimes.com
202 W. 1st Street, Los Angeles, CA 90012
Phone: (213) 237-5000
Email: form on website under 'contact us'

New York Times - www.nytimes.com
620 8th Ave., New York, NY 10018
Phone: 212-556-1234
D.C. Bureau phone: 202-862-0300

Letters to the Editor (for publication): letters@nytimes.com
Write to the news editors: news-tips@nytimes.com
Corrections: nytnews@nytimes.com
Public Editor: public@nytimes.com

USA Today - www.usatoday.com
7950 Jones Branch Dr., McLean, VA 22108-0605
Phone: 703-854-3400
Corrections: accuracy@usatoday.com
Email: form on website under 'contact us'

The Wall Street Journal - www.wsj.com
1211 Avenue of the Americas, New York, NY 10036
Phone: 212-416-2000
Letters to the Editor: wsj.ltrs@wsj.com
Comment on News Articles: newseditors@wsj.com

The Washington Post - www.washingtonpost.com
1150 15th St., NW, Washington, DC 20071-0070
Phone: 202-334-6000
Letters to the Editor: letters@washpost.com
Reader Representative: readers@washpost.com
Email: form on website under 'contact us'

Magazines

The Atlantic - www.theatlantic.com
600 New Hampshire Avenue, NW, Washington, DC 20037
Phone: 202-266-6000
Letters: letters@theatlantic.com

The New Yorker - www.newyorker.com
Four Times Square, New York, NY 10036
Phone: 212-286-2860
Letters to the Editor: themail@newyorker.com

Newsweek - www.newsweek.com
7 Hanover Square, 5th Floor New York, NY 10004
646-867-7100
Email: form on website under 'contact us'

Time – www.time.com
Time & Life Building, Rockefeller Center, 1271 Avenue of the
Americas, New York, NY 10020-1393
Phone: 212-522-1212
Letters to the Editor: letters@time.com

News Services/Wires

Associated Press - www.ap.org
450 West 33rd St., New York, NY 10001
Phone: 212-621-1500
General Questions and Comments: info@ap.org

Reuters - www.reuters.com
3 Times Square, New York, NY 10036

Telephone: 646-223-4000
Email: form on website under 'contact us'

United Press International - www.upi.com
1133 19th Street, NW, Suite 800, Washington, DC 20036
Telephone: 202-898-8000
Email: form on website under 'contact us'

FAIR wants to hear about your media activism. If you write to a media outlet, you can share a copy with FAIR:

FAIR
124 West 30th Street, Suite 201
New York, NY 10001
fair@fair.org

Do's and Don'ts

DON'T

- Swear – Even though it may feel %*@#! great to use profanity in your letter, don't. At best your letter will be ignored. At worst, the Secret Service could show up at your door.

- Demand a response

- Write disrespectfully

DO

- Say who you are – No name equals no consideration

- Write with respect

- Kindly request a response

- State the purpose of your letter in clear, simple terms

- Include paper evidence or cite specific examples to support your position when necessary

- Tell them what it is you want done or recommend a course of action to be considered

- Thank the person for reading your letter

Parting words:

What do you do if someone calls you about your letter or returns your call? Read the last paragraph of the letter you wrote to remind yourself what outcome you were hoping for, and then say it again. Remember they are people just like you; so how do you talk to another person? Like a person.

The Election Process

The condensed version for very busy people

Every 4 years we elect a new president. Candidates from major and minor political parties and independent candidates raise money and campaign for about a year before the General Election. In order to officially represent any political party, the candidate must be nominated by that party. The nominating process officially begins with the state primaries and caucuses, which typically occur in February of an election year, and continue through June. Registered voters vote in primaries or participate in caucuses. Some candidates move forward, some are forced out due to lack of money or support. Independents have no formal support from a party and so they will need millions and millions of dollars, plus millions of signatures to even get a shot at being on a ballot. Public perception is heavily influenced by the media, public opinion polls, surveys and advertising of all kinds. These things are there to highlight a candidate's (and his/her party's) perceived strengths and weaknesses.

In the spring, candidates campaign tirelessly for primaries and caucuses across the country. This part of the election process comes to an end at the national conventions for the political parties. Once the convention arrives (late summer of the election year), the delegates from the states cast votes for the person who will represent their political party in the general election (held in November of the election year). These delegates vote until one candidate receives the majority of the votes. Once a candidate is chosen that candidate then has to pick a running mate, the Vice Presidential candidate. In general the VP is chosen based on his/her ability to balance the ticket. This could mean someone who is very popular in a state or states where the presidential candidate is NOT, or it could be someone who has more experience on something than the presidential candidate, making the whole package more attractive. If the current president is running for re-election, the nomination process will still be completed and the national convention will still occur.

The primary process ends and the general election officially begins the night of the conventions. All the squabbling and the infighting among the parties typically comes to an abrupt end, and the whole party 'unifies,' putting all of their concentrated efforts into getting their party's choice elected.

Those who chose to run without party affiliation have a more difficult road. They don't have to worry about getting their party's nomination, but they must file a declaration of candidacy and a certification of his/her selection for vice president with the secretary of state for EVERY STATE. They are then charged with the nearly impossible task of collecting millions of signatures to support their nominations before they are allowed to run in the general election. This requires staff, money, and time. Unlike the parties who can hit the ground running, independents cannot file a petition nor circulate a certificate of nomination until January of the election year. They also do not have access to the deep financial pockets of a political party, so their funding must come from personal wealth, fundraising campaigns, and loans.

Candidates campaign up to and including Election Day, crisscrossing the country over and over, making public appearances, giving speeches and raising funds. To help get their message across and win our votes, they use advertising, the media, direct mailings, robo calls, human calls, and anything else they can think of to get us to vote for them.

We vote on Election Day and a president is elected.

The end.

For those who need just a little more information...

Let's break it down:

Hi. I heard you were looking to hire a president for the United States of America. May I have an application, please?

While the qualifications to apply for the job of president are simple (a natural-born U.S. Citizen, at Least 35 years old and a U.S. resident for at least 14 years), the road to becoming the president is much harder... and longer... and very, very expensive.

Consider the election process as a job interview. We voters are like members of the board of directors looking to hire the right person for the position we are trying to fill. No matter what, this is the general idea of the election process for the candidate:

- Get your name on the ballot.
- Tell people about yourself and why you are the best choice.
- On Election Day wait while people cast their votes.
- Become the next president or be turned down for the job

Ballot: The voting paper for a vote made in secret.

Our job is to vote someone in. But that's before we toss in platforms, the electorate, primaries, caucuses, conventions, campaign strategies and money, Money, MONEY! Does the candidate have the financial backing, the following, and the stomach for the mother of all job interviews? The election process can be a tricky experience for the candidate and voters alike, but understanding how the election process works can make it all a lot easier for us, the voters. When you strip away the name calling and the media coverage, each of us has only one thing to do in this election, and that is to cast our vote. If you want to get more involved (join a campaign, hang a sign in your car window, etc.) that's great, but all the frenzy is about one thing and one thing only – You and me casting our votes for president.

So, Presidential Hopeful, tell me a little about yourself: Why do you want this job?

We have different goals as voters than presidential hopefuls have as candidates. We are trying to find the best person for the job and the candidate is trying to win an election. Enter 'campaign strategy.' The first thing a candidate must do (assuming he/she has already put together a staff and chosen a campaign manager) is to pick a platform – 'Where will I stand on the issues?' If they want to connect with the voters and be taken seriously by the media, they have to decide what issues to focus on. A candidate needs to stand out among all of the others. Think of those eye catching slogans and big campaign promises as lights on the Las Vegas Strip – the whole point of the Vegas triple "B" (Big Bling that Blinks) is to get you to come in and check them out. Keep in mind, any major policy a candidate puts up during the election ("I'm going to fix education!" "I'm going to create jobs!...") is going to have to go through congress once he/she is in office, and congress "dudn't do nuttin' " until they are good and ready. In many cases campaign promises are more like over-hyped wish lists.

Political Platform: A document stating the aims and principles of a political party.

Hook: That thing or piece of information that draws people in. It can also highlight the type of candidate they are going to run as. Examples: "The progressive candidate.' "The moderate." "The conservative," and so on.

On with the Show! I mean Campaign. That's right, Campaign!

They have their 'platform' and they have their 'hook.' Now what? They are officially running for president! And so begins the dog and pony show, or in this case, the elephant and donkey show.

Part of being a 'free' nation is the right to decide who stays and who goes. With the president we do it every four years. While it would be refreshing to simply go over the candidate's resume, call references and run an interview, this country is way too big for something so intimate. Instead, presidential hopefuls must find another way to get our vote. This happens in the form of campaigning. This is no picnic for them, either. They have to run all over the country yelling, "Look at me! Hire me!" They have to eat cold pizza night after night, live out of a suitcase, and spend their days on a stage, in a plane or working late from a bus, all while watching their money fly out the window faster than they can raise it.

As everything begins and ends with money, a serious contender would need to raise a boatload of cash. So the question becomes: Is it worth it? To find that out, an Exploratory Committee would come together. If they say you are good to go, then you'd amass a campaign team and staff, and you'd be ready to launch your political campaign

Exploratory Committee: A group created to help decide if a potential candidate should run.

Political Campaign: A race between candidates for elective office.

Core Campaign Staff: The most important people in an organization working to get a candidate elected.

Campaign Manager: Does exactly what the title says, which is to manage the campaign itself.

Chief Fundraiser: This person is supposed to 'Show you the money!'

Press Secretary: This person manages the relationship between the candidate and the media, doing his/her best to keep a consistent message and positive information flowing the candidate's way.

Online Communications: This group is charged with handling the candidate's website and all things 'online,' such as You Tube, Facebook, Twitter, Blogging, Search Engine Optimization and more.

Pollsters: The folks who conduct polls to get data on everything from testing the validity of the candidate's message, to finding out which color jacket he/she should wear to appear the most trustworthy.

Consultants: These people are advisors for every topic of the campaign: Money, strategy, advertising, the message, and much more.

Then You Announce:

Dear Country,

Please join me in my candidacy for the presidency. RSVP ASAP with your $25 donation check written to...

Grab an ax, chop down a tree and start Stumpin!'

The stump speech is a political campaign speech made on the campaign trail, dating back to when candidates would stand on a tree stump so they could be heard while they talked. This speech is made over and over again during the primary campaign, then again during the general election. The stump speech will include pieces of their platform and their hook.

Campaign Trail: Planned events in different places that are taken part in, or given by a candidate who is trying to get elected.

Platform: A document stating the goals and principles of a political party.

WOW! It's almost time for the Primaries. Are you still in the race?

If a candidate fails to attract enough money and support to mount a competitive race to the finish line, the smart thing to do is to walk away before the campaign falls further into debt. For those who are left standing, the road only gets rougher, and the stakes only get higher.

The Primary Election is an election that takes place within a party, before the general election. This is where voters cast their vote for the person they want to represent their party in the General Election. This is how we dwindle the 17 men and women running for the Republican nomination down to 1 on the ballot for the General Election. Some states do not have a primary, they have a caucus, but the end result is the same. Whoever wins this election will become the presidential candidate for their party in the General Election. When you hear people talk about 'The Primaries' or 'The Caucuses' they are talking about this election.

There are a few other obscure kinds, but the three main types of primaries are Closed, Open or Semi-Closed. You may have to be registered with a party in order to cast a vote or you may only have to be a registered voter. Some states even let you change your party affiliation at the polls on voting day.

If you are to pick a party your voter registration form will have a space for 'Party Affiliation.' If you do not have to pick a party there will be no mention of a party on your voter registration form. If you are hesitant to vote in a primary because you are unsure, don't let that keep you from voting. Instead, call or email your County Clerk, Election Division and they will clear up any confusion. Many counties even have a Community Services Department in the Election Division. They enjoy calls from people who are looking to involve themselves in the process.

On the date of your state's Primary Election you simply go to your polling place. If your state is Closed, they will hand you the ballot for your party. If your state is Open, they will ask you which ballot you want (The Democrats or the Republicans). In a Semi-Closed, those who are registered as a Democrat or a Republican will automatically receive that ballot, but those people who did not pick a party are allowed to choose which one they want.

Primary: A preliminary election to appoint delegates to a party conference or to select the candidates for a principal, especially presidential, election. Here your vote is secret.

Caucus: Where voters in each precinct come together to discuss the candidates, then make their choice. The results are tallied and sent into party headquarters. Vote counting is done by the parties, not government officials. Here your vote is very public.

Open Primary: A Primary election in which voters are not required to declare party affiliation.

Closed Primary: A Primary election in which only voters registered for the party which is holding the primary may vote.

Semi-Closed Primary: In a semi-closed primary, unaffiliated voters may choose which party primary to vote in, while voters registered with a party may only vote in that party's primary.

More What the $%@#

I know it seems obvious that the point of a primary or a caucus is for we voters to vote for who we want to run in the general election, but that's not so. Sigh... The point of a primary and a caucus is to select delegates to the parties' national conventions. So even though you may be checking off the candidate of your choice on the ballot, you are actually voting for delegates who support that candidate. Those delegates will go to the national convention representing your (the voter's) choice. That may change if no one candidate has enough delegates to win. When that happens they take a delegate vote over and over until someone does have enough delegate support to win the party's nomination to run in the General Election.

Party Crashers

The Republican and Democrat candidates have it easy, because states automatically put them on the election ballot. Independent candidates don't have a party... or a war chest... or the support of the government to make things happen. They must petition each state to be on the ballot. States may require a potential candidate to get a large number of voter signatures, pay steep filing fees, and follow lots of complicated procedures before he or she can get on the ballot. To get on the presidential ballot in all 50 states requires millions of dollars, signatures, and additional thousands in filing fees.

Nomination of the VP

There is no set rule for when a candidate for Vice President is added to the ticket of a presidential candidate. It typically happens after the primaries and caucuses, but before the National Convention. The reason for this is that the V.P. is often someone who was running for president, but either dropped out of the race or lost the primary election.

Ticket: Another name for ballot.

National Convention

A United States presidential nominating convention is a political convention held every four years in the United States by Republicans and Democrats. In many ways these conventions are the same as a regular convention. There are breakout sessions, classes, lectures, meetings, bad food, late night parties and more. Parties adopt the party's official platform for the next four years, and outline the rules for the party's activities, including the presidential nominating process for the next election cycle. The national convention is also where the nominee for Vice President is confirmed and announced. The most important thing that happens at these conventions is the roll out of the top and bottom of the ticket (Top = Presidential Candidate. Bottom = Vice Presidential Candidate).

Ahhh, the Happy Couple

It's magical when presentation and image get together. There is an official power team! The President and Vice Presidential candidates for the party have been named. Let the confetti fly! Finally we enter the fun part of elections: The theatre! The pageantry! Life is a stage and we are but players! Let's dim the lights, strike up the band and cue the actors: Campaigns as Broadway musicals! Did you pick up your t-shirt and soundtrack in the lobby? Flashy campaigns are a lot more important to us than we'd like to admit. Politicians and big businesses play to that.

The Keynote Address

This is considered a highlight of the convention. A prominent or up-and-coming politician in the party delivers a speech designed to rally the party and convey the platform for the election in a persuasive way. Keep an eye out for who was chosen and why. The keynote might have been chosen to help collect votes from a state the party is trying to win over. Additionally, they could be looking to focus on a group of voters they are trying to reach such as minorities, women or young people.

The Presidential Nominee's Acceptance Speech

Along with every other speech they will give for the length of the campaign, this speech is considered to be THE MOST important speech of the campaign. The nominating speech will be different than the one they gave along the campaign trail. Not only different because it sets the tone for the Fall election, but it will lay out priority issues and identify key differences between the candidate and his/her opponent.

The Democratic National Convention will be held at the Wells Fargo Center in Philadelphia, Pennsylvania, from July 25-28, 2016.

The Republican National Convention will be held at the Quicken Loans Arena (called "The Q") in Cleveland, Ohio, from July 18-21, 2016.

Money Stuffs

Who pays for these conventions? Federal funds from the federal treasury are provided for the major parties through the Federal Election Campaign Act. As if $15 million wasn't enough, the FEC

(Federal Election Commission) allowed special interest groups to 'donate' as much money as they wanted to the "host committees" in charge of running the conventions. Donating to a "host committee" is a way for corporations and unions to legally give large unchecked amounts of money to the parties. Lobbying is how we are heard. Money equals lobbying. Individuals (that's us) are allowed to donate up to $2500 to a candidate. These special interest groups are able to put themselves in a position to be heard 1000% louder and clearer than you and me, *The People*. So for every $1 the average American spends on an election, lobbyists (soft money) spend about $10,000.

Political Convention: A formal meeting of members, representatives, or delegates of a political party.

Lobbying: Seeking to influence a politician or public official on an issue.

Lobbyist: Someone hired by a business or a cause to persuade legislators to support that business or cause. They are paid to win favor from politicians.

Free Country: Sour Grapes

Anyone running for president in any of the other parties is not a part of this process at all. All the hype and the media attention (and the money) goes to the Democrats and the Republicans. One of the other candidates from the other parties might be the best candidate for the job, but they aren't part of the glitterati and you'll be lucky to hear their names, let alone what they have to say. You certainly won't see them at 'the debates.' Please remember that while you can't vote for them in a primary or a caucus, it is the General Election and the General Election alone that determines who the next president will be. There are always more than two candidates running for president.

Debates: A formal discussion on a topic in a public meeting or government gathering, where conflicting arguments are put forward.

We all remember the names Obama, Romney, Biden and Ryan, but do any of these names sound familiar from four years ago?

- Gary Johnson
- Jill Stein
- Rocky Anderson
- Virgil Goode

Never heard of them, right? Me neither. And these are people who had significant ballot status. Many more people ran who were only on the ballot in a few states. In this country, money makes you more qualified to lead the country. Not having a war chest big enough to rebuild a third world country makes you less qualified for the job of President. FYI – George Washington was always broke. I'm just sayin.'

Ballot Status: Candidates who had their names on the ballot for many or most states.

The Glitterati are Getting Squeezed too

Even within the Republican and Democratic parties the best candidate might not make it to the primary if his/her war chest isn't deep enough. Primaries/Caucuses used to be spaced out from the new-year through June. This allowed candidates who didn't have tons-o-cash to build a following one state at a time. They were able to create financial backing and get media coverage/interviews. This is what gave them a legitimate shot at winning the primary. The only candidates who could handle a financially tight schedule were the ones with a whole lot of cash, and since that kind of money has a tendency to come from big business with private agendas, that's not really the ideal situation for a country designed to be of the people, by the people, for the people... which includes those us without millions of dollars.

The Winds of Change: Enter **www.Americanselect.org.** Their motto: Pick a President, Not a Party. I'm pointing them out, because the people who created this website stood up and tried to hold a nationwide online primary of their own in 2012. They were trying to put a non-Republican, non-Democrat on the ballot in all 50 states. They believe that the ballot access laws have unjustly restricted the choices available to you and me, and have put third party candidates and candidates who are not affiliated with an established party at a disadvantage.

Third Party Candidate: Any and all political parties in the United States other than the Republican and Democratic Party. The term can also refer to independent politicians not affiliated with any party at all and to write-in candidates.

This group did not get enough visibility last time, but came very close on their first try. They have already laid the groundwork and gained a following of more than four million people. They also let national and local media know they have a mission: They are going to create more choice in our political system so that candidates unaffiliated with the nominating process of either major party will have an authentic way to run for office. And this is going to give you and me, The People, a bigger voice in our political process. Hats off to AmericansElect.org! In 2016 we will have a third person to vote for on the presidential ballot. Does that mean he/she will be the best choice? Well, that will be up to each of us to decide. Never doubt that a small group of people can change the world, because they are working to do just that. If you are interested in a third party candidate, head to their website and sign up.

Politicians don't spend their time running things as much as they spend time running *for* things. Accepting that reality makes it easier to understand all that comes after, such as why Big Money, special interest groups, and high paid lobbyists wield so much power. Such as why robo calls and attack ads dominate all forms of media for a year. In general, when we regular humans are hired for jobs, we get to keep them, and they become ours to lose. If politicians want to keep their jobs, they basically have to PAY to stay. The Congressman, Senator or President who spends all of his or her time diligently and zealously doing the work of the American people will not be a Congressman, Senator or President for long. Raising money is a constant burden that can take more than 50% of their time. During an election year it's most of the job. After all, if you can't keep your job, how will you DO your job?

It wasn't the intention of the framers, but in the political world it is more important to be a good fundraiser than to be a good candidate. Money equals contacts, staff, advertising, and influence. "He who has a thing to sell and goes and whispers in a well is not so apt to get the dollars as he who climbs the tree and hollers." Climbing that tree is expensive. The war chests for Obama and Romney were filled with hundreds and hundreds of millions of dollars.

Compassion Alert: Please don't feel sorry for presidential candidates, congressmen/women or senators. If they wanted to change how campaigns function in this country well, um… they make the laws.

Our challenge is to look beyond:

There is technical stuff, behind the scenes stuff, and stuff that gets pretzeled by the misinformation of the media machine. It's not as hard as it may seem to untwist the pretzel and do what we came here to do: Choose a president. We need only to look beyond the money, beyond gender, beyond disability, beyond race, beyond creed, beyond the resume, beyond the attack ads, beyond the coverage, and beyond the media. In short: We need to look beyond the donkey and elephant show.

What truly matters is the position we are trying to fill. That means our individual criteria is all we should use to judge the candidate. And that criteria is our individual body of opinions – where we stand on the issues. The candidate needs to speak to your body of opinions, your issues. What do you think of the candidate for the position you are trying to fill? Judge them on their merits, their stand on the issues, their ability to communicate. Once you know what you are looking for, the craziness of the election will fall away.

Note: The General Election is November 8, 2016 and this is where we will cast our vote for president.

Welcome to the General Election!

From this point on, it's anybody's ballgame! The Green Party, the Tea Party, the D's, The R's, the I's and the L's are all candidates for the job.

DISCLAIMER: Things seem to be changing rapidly, and while I hope that the 2016 election finds many good candidates getting the chance to be heard, this section is going to focus on the election process involving the two dominant parties – Republicans and Democrats. I will include some direction on tracking down information about third party candidates.

Political Campaign for the General Election

The candidate is on the general election ballot and all that's left is to win! Or lose. The results depend on how effective the campaign was in comparison to the other candidate. An effective campaign requires a solid strategy that can change with the political climate. Understanding that climate requires the campaign team to constantly pay attention to what's happening in the media and with the voters. We'd like them to get that information by sitting down at a coffee shop and talking with us directly. It would be nice if we regular folks could speak our minds and ask questions based on our concerns away from the hype. Assuming they ask the right questions, polling may be able to give them the kind of insight they might have gotten at that coffee shop.

Political Climate: The change in mood and opinions of the people about political issues.

POLLS

The word "poll" means to analyze information, by taking a sample of opinions on a subject gathered from specific or random groups of people. When a political poll is used correctly, it measures the opinions of the group in order to determine the probable opinions of a specific population. Translation: We voters are watered down to a number and a label that helps strategists design a plan to win our vote. Single mothers of 1.5 children respond to... Married men, ages 47-54 resonate with... College students ages 18-22 want to hear more about... There are many different kinds of polls, and while they may be used a great deal during the campaign, their reported results don't have to have any bearing on our decisions or our thoughts. A poll is meaningless in comparison to our own thoughts and opinions.

Strategist: A person skilled in planning action or policy, especially in war or politics.

There are many different kinds of polls to be aware of. Below are a few:

Push Poll: This is when a political campaign tries to influence or change the view of the person they are asking questions of disguised as an unbiased poll. A large number of people are contacted, and very little, if any, effort is made to collect and analyze the response information. It's more like a form of telemarketing based on rumors and propaganda made to look and feel like a poll. So basically a question might sound like this: "If you were made aware that your candidate was mentally unstable would you be more likely to vote for her or less likely?" You were NOT just told that the candidate is unstable. You were just asked to render an opinion on a situation that doesn't exist, meant to sway you into thinking that your candidate just might have a concealed mental illness. That's a push poll.

Random Sampling:

Names and contact information are chosen from a list generated randomly or from specific criteria to represent the entire population of a certain area. It could also be to represent a certain type of person (soccer mom, young male/female professional, college student, retiree, middle class income, lower class income, drinks coffee, eats peas, likes Pina Coladas and gettin' caught in the rain... you get the idea). Their list is made more random by having the caller only reach out to every third or ninth person on that list in order to keep it as random as possible. These lucky people are then contacted, typically by phone (during the dinner hour), and asked specific questions of their thoughts and personal beliefs on a topic. They collect your data and it's used to decide something and/or to hold up to the general public as a representation of what is going on with all of us who fit that type of person or live in that area.

Gallup: A public opinion poll. Although originated by Dr. George Gallup, the term has taken on a more generic meaning. It is a sampling of public opinion or public awareness concerning a certain subject or issue. The same process as the others is used, and then we get told what our opinion is based on that poll.

Interesting Fun Fact: We voters do a strange thing regarding polls. We generally believe the results of a poll, but we don't believe in the scientific principles a poll is based on. So we say in general polls do a good job of predicting elections, and that they are accurate when used to measure 'public opinion' on other issues. However, we simultaneously don't believe that a survey of 1,500 – 2,000 people can accurately represent the views of all Americans. How is it that we can have no confidence in the methods used to get the answers, but can have lots of confidence in the answers themselves? Sometimes we Americans are goofy.

Remember this now and always: Polls are easily manipulated to create the illusion of accuracy... So always apply your own logic.

Poll results can bring endorsements, headlines, and money to a candidate, and can equally sway those things away. When you hear, "according to a recent poll," stop and apply your own logic to the moment. Numbers lie all the time. Numbers can reflect that the candidate's message isn't well received, or it could mean the candidate's message isn't being heard, or it could mean that the candidate's message wasn't understood. All of these are distinctly different meanings that could easily be assumed from the same poll numbers.

If you want to consider a poll, use these questions:

- Who's 'they?' Who paid for or sponsored the poll?

- How were the questions worded? Wording can easily skew the results. Let's say you are asked what you think the most important issue is to you, but the issue that truly is the most important to you wasn't one of the choices. Is that poll still correct?

- When did they do this survey? The numbers are likely to reflect the current political climate. If that poll was months ago or days ago, but the climate has changed then it's not timely and therefore less accurate. An example would be a poll taken about concern about terrorism on American soil the day before 9/11, and a poll taken the day after 9/11.

- Who did they survey? Were the participants people like me? Results shift radically depending on who is polled on what.

- Did 'they' mention their margin of error? Any poll worth taking a look at will provide the margin of error. Lets say it's 5%. Well, if the topic shows a difference of 5% (such as how far ahead one candidate is over another... that really means that it's just as likely they are running neck and neck.

Margin of Error: The error that occurs simply because the researchers aren't asking everyone. The margin of error is supposed to measure the maximum amount by which the sample results are expected to differ from those of the actual population. Because the results of most survey questions can be reported in terms of percentages, the margin of error most often appears as a percentage, as well.

Pack up some laundry quarters and your mini fridge 'cuz we're off to college! The Electoral College

So, umm... ... well, we don't actually 'vote' for the president. We vote for Electors, who are part of the Electoral College.

The Election Process

The Electoral College is not a place you drive to. It is a process outlined in the Constitution. A group of people called "electors," are generally selected by the political parties in each state. Though this is not true of every state, it is mostly the case that each candidate will have their own set of potential electors in that state. So, the Republicans have their electors on standby and the Democrats have their electors on standby. On election day we Americans cast our votes. If 52% of Illinois votes for a Democrat then the electors of the Democratic party in Illinois come forward and cast their vote for the Democrat.

Huh?

What were the framers smokin' when they came up with this one?! In this instance, they were worried that We, The People would either be uninterested or unable to learn about the different candidates who might be running (this being long before TV, the telephone, Google). They were also concerned about small states ending up with little to no say because of their size. This was their way of making it more equal and so a math genius came up with the Electoral College.

FYI: Though the founding fathers thought electors would learn about the candidates for us and then vote, it doesn't really work that way. There is no federal law requiring Electors to vote according to the results of the popular vote, but Electors are typically bound by either a state law, pledges made to political parties or both. The people chosen to be Electors are usually picked because they hold a leadership role in their party, or because they have years of loyal service to the party under their belts. So the concern is less about electors and more about the 'winner take all' notion.

When Al Gore received 50,999,897 votes and George W. Bush received 50,456,002 votes, Al Gore won by 543,895 votes… but he was not elected president. Al Gore won the popular vote, but we use the Electoral College, which is 'winner take all' state per state.

Popular Vote: The vote for the President of the United States made by qualified voters and not by elected officials.

Elector: A member of the electoral college.

State Party Convention: A party meeting held every two years for the purpose of nominating candidates for statewide office, adopting a platform, electing the party's leadership, and in presidential election years selecting delegates for the national convention and choosing presidential electors.

How many Electors does my state get?

The number of electors a state gets is based on the number of people it has in congress: Which is the number of Senators and Congressmen for that state. Each state has 2 senators. The number of Congressmen is different for every state. They are assigned based on the number of districts in a state, and the districts are based on population. If you want to know how many electoral votes your state has refer to the map in this section.

Electoral Math

With limited time and even more limited funds, candidates are forced to target their campaign to specific states or regions. Polling and the electoral map dictate how they will proceed. If we want to understand more about this process we'll need a quick math lesson. There are 538 possible votes that can be won by a presidential candidate. Once a candidate wins 270 electoral votes he or she has won the election.

Here's the Breakdown: There are 435 representatives in the House of Representatives and 100 Senators in the Senate. The 23rd amendment to the Constitution gave 3 electoral votes to Washington D.C. ('cuz they didn't get to vote before) bringing the total of electoral votes to 538. The first candidate to receive 270 votes wins the presidency: Why? Because 538 divided in half equals 269. To win you must get one more vote than half. 269+1=270.

Electoral Math: Adding up the votes of a bunch of states you think you can win in to see if you've made it to 270. It helps the candidate see what states they need to focus on so they can win the election.

Time for a little finger painting:

Blue States: These are states that have a long history of voting for the Democrats.

Red States: These are states that have a long history of voting for Republicans.

Purple: States that might go either way. Swing states. Get it? Red and Blue make Purple.

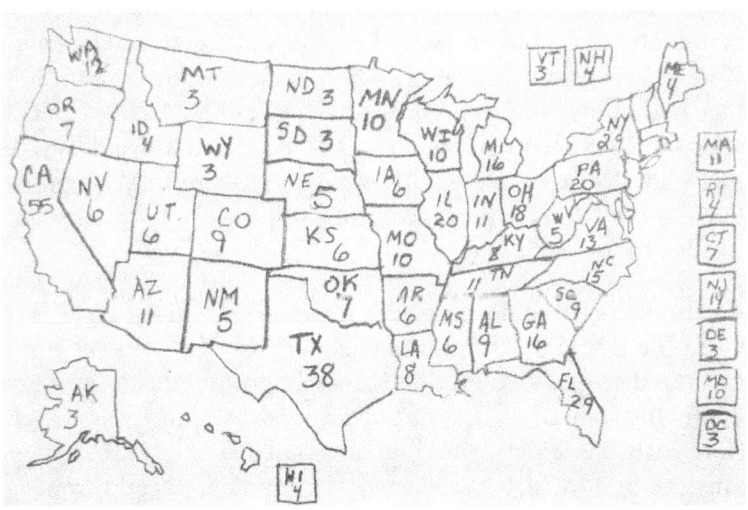

Swing States (or Battleground States): States where the two major political parties have about the same levels of support among voters, and are also viewed as important in determining the overall result of a presidential election.

Total Electoral Votes possible: 538
Total a candidate needs to win: 270

A Few Things We Need To Know About On The Campaign Trail:

Buzz Words: The media and candidates use a lot of words everyday that say a little, but mean a lot. Beware of these words. An example is 'Job Creators.' When candidates talk about Job Creators they are trying to imply that big business is where all the new jobs are going to come from. Without question, we are supposed to believe wealthy businesses are going to save us, just because someone used the words 'Job Creators' in a sentence. If we stop to take it apart though, we'll see that those 'Job Creators' only make up 20% of the American work force. About 80% of this country is made up of small businesses. Wouldn't that make small businesses the actual 'Job Creators?' And do we count how many jobs those big businesses outsourced to other countries? If we do, that would make them 'Job Relocaters.' Are we including the hundreds of thousands of jobs these big businesses cut after the 2008 stock market crash? If we are, that would make them 'Job Deleters.' So, exactly what is 'Job Creators' supposed to mean? We deserve the whole story, not the Cliff's Notes. Buzz words cannot be trusted.

Vetting: To 'Vet' someone means investigate to discover. This is when the media and rival campaigns dig for dirt and skeletons in the other guy's closet. Sometimes important discoveries are made, and sometimes they just make good TV. Either way, it is effective when attempting to discredit someone or to raise ratings. This can be a tough experience for the candidates, and throwing these issues out as 'red meat' to the media is how things can get out of control.

Red Meat: Somehow members of the media needing more and more to report on makes it okay to behave like wild animals. Red Meat is what you feed hungry, man-eating lions. You want to give the media plenty of red meat to focus on so they don't start digging for something juicy to feed upon. Hard to be fair and accurate when you are ravenous for a story, any story. Why is this behavior okay?

Wedge Issues: An issue that divides or causes conflict in an otherwise unified group. The Democrats and the Republicans look for issues that appeal to we voters, while making the other candidate look like a bad choice. An example would be if the Republicans wanted to ban chocolate and the Democrats believed in our right to eat truffles. Or let's say the Democrats were against coffee and Republicans were all about espresso.

Going Negative

What we want: A zealous critique of another candidate's ideas and policies.

What we get: Attacking the other candidate's competence, character and clothing.

Fun Fact: Candidates do not think it makes them look bad when they say awful things about 'the other guy.' The theory seems to be that attacking the opponent allows voters to see the attacker as the best choice.

4 Roads to Victory

Your vote is competed over in every arena possible so which one speaks to you?

Grassroots

This is where small groups of people, with a little direction from the campaign leaders, go door to door, stuff mailers or make phone calls to others in their district to encourage them to support a specific candidate and to vote.

Couch potato and Drive timers

This is pure advertisement. Hundreds of millions of dollars are spent on these advertisements placed on the radio, TV, internet, billboards and in newspapers. The focus is to give the candidate massive exposure by coming right into our homes and cars with a carefully designed message.

Live and in person for one night only!

'On the Ground' campaigning is where the candidate and as many marketable supporters as can be found (Specific party leaders, family of the candidate, celebrities, etc.) make appearances and give speeches throughout the country in the hopes that a camera will capture it and put them on TV. With media coverage as the goal, advance teams are sent out, sets are designed and cheering crowds with signs and flags and banners are put together.

Bloggers and websites and Facebook, OH MY!

This type of campaigning is an ever changing one, requiring candidates to find and hire staffers who are at once fluent in communication as well as politically savvy. These people spend the entire campaign sitting at a desk monitoring the net, updating the candidate's website, responding to information on the blogosphere to make his/her candidate look good, and finding as many "friends" for the candidate as they can.

Carry a state: To win the state.

Blogosphere: Can refer to the internet, but mainly refers to the notion that all blogs (and bloggers) are connected to each other.

Billy Joel was right: *We didn't start the fire.* Money fueled this inferno.

It keeps coming back to cashola. The Federal Election Campaigning Act established the rules for presidential campaign financing. It requires candidates to create national organizations to handle campaign contributions and expenditures. This paved the way for the organizations to become more professional, which found them relying on political consultants, media experts, and pollsters to plot strategy and provide information and advice.

Mounting a serious campaign for president has become about appealing to those with millions of dollars, leaving the general American public out. The other big problem is the PAC's – Political Action Committees. Business corporations and labor unions can't donate to candidates or spend their own money on campaigns. Fortunately for them, they are allowed to form a PAC. This allows them to contribute millions of dollars to candidates, contribute to parties, and/or to run their own ads without breaking the law. Say hello to corporate lobbyists, special interest groups, and their very deep pockets.

Soft Money: Political donations made in such a way as to avoid federal regulations or limits, as by donating to a party organization rather than to a particular candidate or campaign.

Hard Money: Money given directly to a candidate in an election to assist his or her campaign.

Corporate Lobbying: When the corporations and firms in the country try to influence business and government leaders to create legislation or conduct an activity that will help their organization.

Special Interest Group: Is a group with an interest in advancing solutions to issues. They may at times also advocate or lobby on a particular issue or on a range of issues.

Advocacy Group: A pressure group, normally set up for a specific political aim.

It sounds bad, but it doesn't have to be: Campaign dollars aren't votes. Nobody can 'buy' the election. Each registered voter gets just one. If we are thinking for ourselves then they can 'lobby' 'til they turn blue, red or purple and it won't affect our decisions. Campaign dollars aren't votes.

Me The People

The Debates – Do I Gotta Watch'em?

YES. I know. They are a total drag. Unfortunately, it's one of the only times the candidates meet face to face and discuss the issues. The format stinks and makes it feel like we are instead watching two press conferences happening at the same time, but every now and again something important happens, and that can be useful in helping us determine who we think is the best candidate for the job. Though they may not change our already forming opinions, sometimes the moderator does a great job of moving the debate and we learn something helpful.

Moderator: The person running the debate. If you've watched a debate before, it's the person sitting in the middle asking the questions. This person's job is to start and stop the candidates, ask a candidate a question a second time if the candidate dodged it or didn't answer fully, and generally keep the debate moving forward.

On the campaign trail it's easy to call each other names from 1,000 miles away and twist each other's words to please a crowd, but in the debate setting, the name-calling and hair pulling doesn't work too well. We get to hear more of the story and we are more likely to see the ideas and plans of each candidate tested by the other. Not always. Sometimes it dissolves into childish political theater. But hopefully the buzz words and sound bites will take a back seat to an open exchange of ideas.

"Hello Mr. Presidential Hopeful. First, tell me a little about yourself... "

Approach each of the debates with an open mind and definitely with a hearty supply of snacks. To do it right, use this handy dandy debate-watching checklist:

- Quiet space
- Your list of the issues that are important to you
- Two sheets of paper for each candidate in the debate

- Pens, pencils
- Comfy clothes
- Snacks and drinks
- Aspirin (optional)

If you think it will be helpful to watch and discuss the debates with others, then invite a few trusted folks over. Watch them live or record, TiVo, or youtube them (**www.youtube.com**) for later. Being able to start and stop them while you take notes might be helpful, but avoid the repeat trap. Things happen live. Things are said in the moment. When they are played over and over again we begin to assign them more meaning and weight than they deserve. Do your best to keep your first impressions fresh.

Pros and Cons

Create a Pros and Cons list for each candidate. As they speak, note on a sheet of paper what is good and what is not so good in your opinion.

Check Your Emotions

Emotions are good, but use them to think, rather than thinking with them. If you have a general dislike for someone make sure it's because of the issues or your personal feeling on his/her ability to do the job. If it's because the candidate reminds you of someone you couldn't stand back in high school.....not a strong reason to disqualify them.

Parting Words:

'Spin' is worth mentioning twice. The split second each debate ends every news outlet will be talking about it, tearing apart words, phrases, glances, tie color, stance, pauses, breaths, hairdo, and sentence structure. Their personal opinions will always color their media coverage. The debates are personal. You sat there and you watched. If there is something you didn't understand, you can look it up on your own or talk it over with a trusted friend or loved one. Let the pundits ramble while we make up our own minds.

Debate Schedule

To view the 2015/2016 Presidential Primary Debate Schedule:

Go to www.USPresidentialElectionNews.com and click on '2015-2016 Republican Primary Debate Schedule' or '2015-2016 Democratic Primary Debate Schedule.'

To view the 2016 Presidential and Vice Presidential Debate Schedule:

Go to www.USPresidentialElectionNews.com and click on '2016 General Election Debate Schedule.'

Me The People

Look At This Face...
Is This The Face Of A Liar??

Finding Factual Information So We Can Vote With Confidence

How can good information be found? Is there even such a thing as good information? You have options. The problem in the 'information age' is *not* information. We are bombarded with TMI – 'Too Much Information.' The problem is gaining access to reliable information and being able to make sense of it; that which is trustworthy, unbiased and accurate.

I am sorry to say that at the end of the day there is no place to find completely unbiased or totally factual information about anything. The goal is to get as close as you can so that you feel comfortable comparing and contrasting the information with your own body of opinions. As there is a constant stream of contradiction, the need to collect quality information from several sources is necessary.

• Watch or listen to news that you trust be it a local or national program.

• Read a newspaper or two that you have faith in be it a local paper or national one.

• Have conversations about topics with people whose opinion you trust and respect.

• Spend time on the internet only at sites you trust to give you information on the candidate, on an issue or on an event that has been reported.

• From time to time listen to and read informed and balanced opinions that differ from or fully disagree with your own.

• Attend a rally to hear the candidate speak.

• Watch the debates.

- Watch a recording of a speech on youtube or on the candidate's website. Be sure to confirm the speech you have selected wasn't edited or 'doctored' by a competitor or a non-fan.

Psst: You can do the same thing for third party candidates, but the information will be a little harder to come by, as they are not receiving as much attention or coverage. Begin at their websites and follow their campaign trail information to help you along.

Below is a list of who is running for President with Significant Ballot Status and internet sources for fact checking and tracking down solid information on candidates and government issues.

Running for President:

- Ben Carson   www.bencarson.com
- Bernie Sanders   www.berniesanders.com
- Chris Christie   www.chrischristie.com
- Hillary Clinton   www.hillaryclinton.com
- Lincoln Chafee   www.chafee2016.com
- John Kasich   www.johnkasich.com
- Lindsey Graham   www.lindseygraham.com
- Carly Fiorina   www.carlyforpresident.com
- Jeb Bush   www.jeb2016.com
- Ted Cruz   www.tedcruz.org
- Jim Gilmore   www.2016.republican-candidates.org
- Mike Huckabee   www.mikehuckabee.com
- Bobby Jindal   www.bobbyjindal.com
- Rand Paul   www.paul.senate.gov
- Marco Rubio   www.marcorubio.com
- Martin O'Malley   www.martinomalley.com
- George Pataki   www.georgepataki.com

- Rick Santorum   www.ricksantorum.com
- Donald Trump   www.donaldjtrump.com
- Jim Webb   www.jameswebb.com
- Scott Walker   www.scottwalker.com

FAIR DIRECTORY

www.NoLabels.org – This is a national citizens organization working to usher in a new era of problem solving in American politics. They are out to shake up the system and compel our national leaders to get back to the business of solving the problems facing the nation.

www.factcheck.org – Another nonpartisan site that checks the accuracy of political ads and allegations. This site is sponsored by the Annenberg Public Policy Center at the University of Pennsylvania.

www.Realclearpolitics.com – This is an independent political web site, meaning it is not designed to serve any one party. It's updated every morning with commentary, news, polling data and links to important resources from all sides of the political world.

www.c-span.org – C-SPAN'S 2016 Vote web page has video of campaign speeches and links to candidate websites. click on **'Road to the White House 2016'**

www.vote411.org – Comprehensive, nonpartisan info on the election and on voting. Stuff like: Registering to vote, rules for absentee ballots and early voting, locating your polling place, and lots more.

www.publicintegrity.org – The Center for Public Integrity is an American nonprofit investigative journalism organization whose stated mission is, "to reveal abuses of power, corruption and dereliction of duty by powerful public and private institutions in order to cause them to operate with honesty, integrity, accountability and to put the public interest first."

www.gop.com – Republican National Committee's official party site. Covers GOP (Government of Power) issues, party platform, party rules, etc.

www.politifact.com – PolitiFact is an independent fact-checking journalism website aimed at bringing the truth in politics. Politi-Fact's reporters and editors fact-check statements from the White House, Congress, candidates, advocacy groups and more, rating claims for accuracy on their Truth-O-Meter. Every fact-check includes analysis of the claim, an explanation of their reasoning and a list of links to all their sources.

www.democrats.org – Democratic National Committee's official party site. Covers issues, party platform, party rules, etc.

www.pollingreport.com – This nonpartisan site has current and past public opinion polling for elections and public policies.

www.lwv.org – The League of Women Voters provides nonpartisan policy information. Also included are links to state and local sites and information about voter registration.

www.presidentialelection.com – This is a non-partisan site that offers factual information on who to vote for, issues and following the campaign money.

www.votesmart.org/voteeasy – Find your political soulmate! One of the THE coolest places to go if you want to sit down and do a side by side comparison of all of the candidates. It's a little like a video game. You click on the issues and how important they are to you. You are matched on each issue with the candidate who most closely matches your opinion.

Candidates don't necessarily want to be nailed down to their EXACT words, and so receiving a full list of their opinions on all the issues is hard to come by. At the national convention the Republicans and Democrats settle on what they are going to put forth and push for during the next four years. To read more about their platforms right from the horses' mouths go to their websites. For the Republicans, go to **www.gop.com** and click on '**Platform**.' For the

Democrats, go to **www.democrats.org** and click on '**Our Party.**' These are only the platforms of the party, and don't necessarily reflect the candidates.

The Knight News Challenge awarded $3.2 million for ideas to better inform voters and increase civic participation before, during and after elections. Twenty-two projects won. Some address the need to provide voters with better information about candidates and issues. Some work to increase voter engagement in the election process. I have highlighted a couple below. If you would like to check out the many others go to **www.knightfoundation.org**, then click on '**22 ideas win Knight News Challenge**.' Most of these tools are available beginning January 1, 2016.

Political Ad Tracker: An online library of all political ads in key 2016 primary regions married with fact checking citizens can trust. Political Ad Tracker is working with leading journalists in the top fact checking organizations (The Center for Public Integrity, Factcheck.org, Politifact.com) to hold candidates accountable for their messaging.

990 Treasure Trove – Dark Money (anonymous money) accounts for hundreds of millions of dollars in each election, but data is hard to come by. The Center for Responsive Politics has created a one of a kind data set that tracks Dark Money spending and probes the complex network through which it flows. This will help voters understand what's happening, hold the groups accountable and make informed decisions about their democracy.

Parting Words:

The best way to fight fire is NOT with fire. It's with Facts.

Votesmart.org.

Me The People

Election DAY is Here!

Election:

An election is a formal decision making process by which a population chooses an individual to hold public office.

What day is today? ELECTION DAY!! This is a profound statement for democracy so it's more than okay to be totally GEEKED, because today is the day. It's time to jump out of bed and cast your vote for the candidate you feel most closely shares your ideals, your hopes and your dreams. It's time to stand behind the person who most embodies what you believe we need to keep our nation strong and safe and free. By the end of the day the election will be over and we can take the *Help Wanted* sign out of the White House window. So Exciting! Below is an unofficial tick-tock of what the day will look like:

- Before you head out, make sure you have the correct ID required by your state (if any).

- Know your polling place.

- If you went through the ballot early, make sure to pack your list of who all you plan to vote for. If you didn't remember to vote with confidence on what you know, and empower yourself to leave things blank that you weren't prepared to vote on.

- Bring a book or something to do in case you need to wait in line to cast your vote. Come prepared for the unexpected. Maybe a snack, a beverage, a folding chair if you have a hard time standing for long periods. Be creative.

- Yes, you can bring your children with you when you vote.

- When you arrive at your polling place it may be quiet and vacant or the area out front may be buzzing with voters, lobbyists and exit poll volunteers. There may be the handing out of pamphlets, cards and other materials. Take what you want and ignore what you don't.

- Step into line and wait for your turn at the table to check in and receive your ballot (When voting by computer you may not receive a paper ballot and will receive a card or number instead).

- Step into your booth or over to the partitioned machine you are led to.

- Follow the instructions and cast your ballot.

- When you are finished bring your ballot, card or number to where you were asked to and then turn it in.

- If your polling place has them, paste on that "I Voted" sticker and walk tall as you exit the building.

- If you are approached and asked who you voted for, feel free to answer or smile and walk away.

- For you it has all come to a timely end. Smile. Today you got to experience a true measure of what it means to be an American!

Snafus and Ballot Blues

I have no idea where my polling place is! Go to www.VOTE411. org and click on '**Polling Place Finder.**' If you don't have internet you can swing by your local library and ask them to look it up for you or call a friend with internet. Remember that you have to go to your designated polling place, because that's where they have your name. If you go just anywhere, they can't let you vote.

I started to vote and I am totally confused:

If you run into any trouble ask for help. That's what the people are there for. It is your right to ask a question, and most people are happy to help you out. If they explain and you still don't get it then ask them to explain it again. If they are not good at it, ask for someone else. People all over the country complain about how difficult the design of these ballots can be sometimes and it's important to get it right.

I am nervous about voting for the first time:

I've been there. Let me say that it's not a judgmental day. People are inning and outing so there is not a lot of chit chat, but rather a lot of 'Happy to be an American' stuff going on. If you think you won't do it alone, then I suggest you vote early so there is no pressure, or take a friend along. You can make a day of it by going with your friend to his/her polling place and then going to yours.

Now, sometimes things go wrong. Ignore the F.E.A.R. impulse (Forget Everything And Run!). Many eligible voters are turned away at the last minute because an Election Judge doesn't know enough or makes a mistake. We're all human. Stand there and politely require the person in charge be brought in to the situation. If you feel intimidated you can show them this page, but don't leave without voting unless the head Election Judge of your polling place has tried to help you, has contacted the County Clerk's election lawyers and yes, has even signed a piece of paper or let you record them stating EXACTLY why you can't vote. This includes the offer of a provisional ballot. Exhaust all options first. Without proof of wrongdoing, you have a constitutional right to be there and to vote the full ballot.

And We THINK The Winner Is:

While exit polls will tell us all day long who they think the winner is, counting the votes is what decides who wins. The media, in an attempt to be clever, as well as keep you glued to their stations, came up with early projections. This means they are literally predicting the outcome of the election WHILE we are still voting. Very un-sportsman like. Should be illegal. The media can in effect discourage people from voting. Don't be influenced by exit polls. The major news networks do this so you'll WATCH THEM, and the candidates and their staff are basically killing time until the actual votes are counted. There is NO OTHER REASON for exit polls. Nothing should sway your vote or sway you from voting so consider turning the TV off on Election Day, at least until you've voted.

This is your day, our day. Why not leave the media out of it? Instead of watching TV, why not call friends and remind them to vote? Why not offer to take a few people who don't have transportation to their polling place? Or wander the streets showing off that "I VOTED" sticker? Or keep people motivated at a long polling line?

And the Winner is:

We have filled the position. *The Help Wanted* sign is off the White House. The winning candidate becomes the President-Elect and holds no official power until sworn in at the inauguration, which happens on January 20th of 2017. You can go back to your normal life with a job well done behind you.

Parting Words:

Some will tell you it's your American duty to stay involved and to be up to speed on every minute detail of politics and government that interests them. Let them say that. Let them do as they please. And you do the same. There are thousands of ways to stay involved and they don't require a militant devotion to watching TV, reading the papers and trolling the net. Stay involved in your own way on your own terms.

After We Have a President

While putting this guide together a woman asked me a question:

If I did everything I was supposed to do and nothing changed then why would I vote again? Let's say that the guy I voted for even won the election and became president, but four years passed and nothing seemed different or any better to me – Why should I ever vote again?

The answer is because that's why we have weekly staff meetings at work: To keep us on track and moving forward. It's why we tell the kids every day for years to make their beds: Because eventually they will do it on their own. It's why we go to school: At first it's hard and it seems we won't get anywhere, but over time we learn and we grow. It's why we work hard at a job that stinks and sucks the life out of us at times: Because eventually there will be a chance to move up in the company and our hard work will pay off. It's why we go to physical therapy after an injury: Every day is a struggle and the progress is so small it can't be seen, but we trust that it will happen over time... and eventually it does.

We should keep voting, because change happens over time. In the government it can happen over 'lots' of time, but with our help and our attention it will happen. I think what she is looking for is to see things change in her world. By the time change trickles down to us from the national government it can feel nonexistent. The solution may be to go another route. Yes, do vote. Yes, do stay informed on the issues that speak to you, but we Americans shine when we make things happen on our own. There is soooooo much change we can make without the government. Instead of trying to change the world, why not to try to make a few changes in 'your world?'

Our local community is our world. Our family and friends are our world. The jobs we hold and the work we do is our world. If you feel like things aren't changing in yours, list out what those things are, then think about which ones you might be able to

115

improve upon. Once you decide, put some of your time, talent and treasure there.

What Can I do?

Help People: You decide what that looks like based on the needs you think you can fill. Check out your Town Hall or community billboard or website for ideas.

Participate in Your Community: You can do all or some – Vote, join a group, attend meetings, support events, create relationships with others. Places to try - Rotary, USO, Boy Scouts, Girls Scouts, School Board, Meals on Wheels. Consider becoming an election judge or a deputy voter registrar.

Be Respectful: Respect takes many forms, but the more we show it to others the more the world around us will improve. You can respect people's time, opinion, choices, privacy, feelings and more. We did this for a while after 9/11, and it made a big difference in morale and emotional recovery.

I suggest you keep a 'Do Good' tally. Raising kids to be great Americans – Good. Anonymously giving money to a struggling family – Good. Working hard at your job to help your company grow and keep people employed – Good. Teaching a seminar on getting out of debt at your local library... Becoming a Brownie or Cub Scout Troop Leader... Going to a city council meeting... Collecting money to buy better equipment for local Police and Fire... That's all doing good! Putting your focus on your world IS being active in politics and government.

Forget the national level. Be a part of your local level. When everyone works to improve their corner of the world, eventually we'll get it all cleaned up together! It's not about time spent. It's about time *well spent*.

After We Have A President

"At first people refuse to believe that a strange new thing can be done, then they begin to hope it can be done, then they see it can be done - then it is done and all the world wonders why it was not done centuries ago."

Frances H. Burnett

Me The People

Appendix: How To Talk About Politics Without Bloodshed

While working on this guide I was fortunate to have met with a professor of Political Science at Depaul University. I was thrilled to tap the brain of this expert. Democracy was in the air! The good Doctor was everything I had hoped for – Smart, energetic, even comical. It was going so well, but just as our synergy kicked in a colleague passed by and was invited to join us... cue Darth Vader's entrance music!

Not only did this professor monopolize the conversation, she couldn't stop telling me what a waste of time this book was. While one professor was excited about seeing more Americans like myself enter into the political world, the other chose to heavily criticize me for daring to think people like me were something other than lazy and worthless. She spouted about my fruitless efforts to create a 'light and easy approach to government and politics.' She was livid that people weren't reading the hundreds of books that are already out there. I politely suggested that the reason they went unread was the complicated and negative way in which those books presented the information. I was cut off mid sentence so I could be told that she held out *'NO hope for my book, because people are apathetic.'* Her take was that if 'they' really wanted to get involved the information is out there and 'they' should be going out and finding it themselves.

I mentally dabbed at the venom dribbling from her chin and said cheerfully, "Your opinion has been heard." I sat in agreeable silence and waited to see what she would do next. To my astonishment she stopped talking. The nastiness she lobbed at me had gone unreturned, leaving her nowhere familiar to go. A few seconds went by and she tried again, this time a little louder. I politely interrupted her and repeated, "As I said, your opinion has been heard." I put my pen down, sat up nice and straight with my hands in my lap and waited again. The cheerful silence was too much for her, because moments later Dr. Darth abruptly excused herself and disappeared. The meeting came to a cordial end. I giggled all the way back to the train having learned two things: One, it was possible to survive a conversational ambush. Two, the next time I met with an expert I would wear a football helmet!

The strange part is I'll bet that professor left thinking she'd given me pearls of wisdom I could use to educate the ignorant masses. Somehow yelling at people for perceived short comings is an accepted way of helping our fellow man. I did learn something from her. People in power and in charge of the information make it too difficult for those of us looking to find help, yet push us to go out and search for it. When we don't, we are called sheep, idiots, and un-American.

Well, let them do that. We don't have to be swayed by those people or be in any way affected by such inappropriate behavior. There are people with whom we can have lively debates and civil discourse. And when the time comes we get to cast our vote the same as they do. This section has ideas on how to shut down the ill mannered folks, and ex- change ideas with the respectful ones.

Civil Discourse: Engagement in discourse (conversation) intended to enhance understanding.

Discourse: Written or spoken communication or debate. Conversation.

Have a Board Meeting

The job of the candidates is to tell us about themselves. Our job is to compare their platform and character to our own body of opinions. We then take that informed opinion and discuss their qualifications with other *board members*. In this case, other board members are fellow Americans. Being able to have an open exchange of ideas or a respectful debate is crucial in our decision making process, but this is where the wheels fall right of the cart for most of us. Well, let's pick up those wheels and build ourselves a sweet new ride!

For now, let's agree that the decision to have a conversation about political issues or about the candidates who are running for president will be limited to talking only with people you find credible, and whose opinions you respect. Share the ground rules with that person so you are both on the same page. And consider that minds are like parachutes. They only work when they are open.

Conversation Ground Rules:

Respect the Other Person. Respect cannot be emphasized enough when dealing with the topic of politics in general, and the Presidential Election in specific.

Avoid White Rabbit Syndrome. Plan enough time to have your conversation. I am not saying that you must have a conversation that lasts an hour, only that starting up a conversation when you don't have the time means that before you know it you are running late for a meeting, picking up kids, getting back to work, etc. Planning time to have a lively and private conversation will allow you to start and finish a topic. This helps avoid misunderstandings and hurt feelings.

Just Say "No" To Electronics. Turn off your cell phone, iPhone, Samsung, iPad, iPod, laptop, notebook, mp3, flat screen and plasma. Constantly having someone's attention diverted to an electronic device of any kind is rude. If you want to call a friend on the phone call them, but do it on your own time. If you want to chat with someone invite that person over, don't text them 26 times while you are out with someone else. Bringing an electronic pacifier into a conversation implies that the person with whom you are talking isn't interesting enough to hold your interest. Show them they are by leaving the electronics alone.

No Real Time Fact Checking. Think of a conversation a bit like a test of your skill and knowledge. Once the conversation begins you are on your own. If you don't know something you don't know it. If your companion has said something you believe to be false, argue it from the information in your head. Under no circumstances do you reach for an electronic referee. It's poor form and incredibly rude to 'fact check' someone during a conversation. First, it's impolite to attempt to prove someone wrong during polite conversation. Second, it's incredibly unkind to put more faith in the internet than in the person you chose to have this conversation with.

People deserve to be free to express an opinion. When someone feels that every word uttered will be subject to the W³ (World Wide Web) then you have failed before you've even begun. When the conversation ends and you have parted ways, feel free to check into anything that didn't ring true for you. If it turns out they were wrong, then that is a topic for another day. And one to be discussed respectfully: "I was looking into a few of the things you mentioned in our last conversation that just didn't feel quite right to me and here is what I found… what are your thoughts on that?"

He'll Have What I'm Having. Avoid assuming that everyone in the room shares your choice of party, your views or your opinions. I had an acquaintance announce to a room full of Democrats that, "When you're 20 if you aren't a Democrat you have no heart. When you're 30 if you're not a Republican you have no brain!" He laughed heartily and didn't know why the entire room was shooting icy daggers at him. He was a nice guy, but no one in the room took the time to find that out. He went home early.

One of These Things Is Not Like The Other. People prepare to ride in to battle on their fiery steed, but not to walk in and sit down for a discussion. For battle all you need is anger, aggression, buzz words and sounds bites. For discussion you need information, thoughtful reflection and the ability to calmly listen and express yourself. Feel free to bring the horse along, but do leave your weapons at home. Consider this: In the military handbook the most successful battle is the battle avoided.

Oh SNAP! That's right. Sometimes people are going to wig out on you. You might have hit a hot button or they felt threatened and reacted. Try as hard as you can to let that be okay. Usually, people spin themselves out quickly and can find their way back to the rational person they were a few minutes ago. Give them the courtesy of letting it go and you may be truly surprised what you learn as a result.

Inquiring Minds Want To Know. Become a reporter by asking probing questions to more fully understand someone's position. There is a temptation to frame the discussion as a 'for or against' debate. When you make it about your individual stories you will each find out what shaped your perspectives. Seeking to understand where someone is coming from is much more satisfying than fruitlessly attempting to change someone's political views.

The most important idea is to keep the conversation going. Whenever you can, connect the topic to everyday life. Facts may be facts, but our opinion of those facts and how we interpret those facts may differ. Focus on those differences. People are not Parties. They are people. Where they stand on issues that are important to them and their opinions about the world we live in is from where you should judge. Care not about their party affiliation, but about where they are coming from. We all deserve someone's effort to listen to us and to seek to understand us.

Leave' em Laughin!' If the last thing said during your conversation was, "Let's agree to disagree," then your entire conversation voided itself out. Tell your conversation companion that you'll look up an article or a poll he/she mentioned, or thank that person for his/her openness. Do your best to end on a positive note. It's just nicer. And it opens the door to more civil discourse down the road.

Danger Will Robinson

If you accidentally find yourself in a political conversation decide whether or not you will proceed. If you want to move forward follow the guidelines above. If you'd rather have a tooth removed without Novocain, below are some ideas on how to make a graceful exit.

Happy to talk about this, but not happy to talk 'now.' You must, must stop the conversation before it gets started. If you allow someone to talk too long before making an exit you risk appearing rude or condescending. Try something such as, "Bob, I apologize for cutting you off and I'd really like to talk more about this another time, but I only talk about stuff like this when I have enough X (Time, Facts, Sleep, etc). I'd like to talk about this with you again sometime and I'm glad you brought it up." This is just one example of how you can steer yourself out of a conversation you don't want to have right now.

Not happy to talk about this topic ever! There is nothing wrong with having taboo topics in your world. There are some things we just don't want to debate or defend. If there are issues and subjects you don't enjoy talking about don't. If people don't respect that, that is their problem not yours. Being respectful as you set your boundaries is the best way to keep it civil. "I'm going to stop you there, Bob. I don't talk about X. I respect you and your opinions, but X is something I do not discuss. Thank you for honoring my choice." If they don't listen repeat it until they do.

Is it me or is it Getting Hot in Here?

Most people have very little experience with civil discourse. In fact, many of us have very little experience with discourse of any kind. Most of us are used to avoiding conversation topics that might cause hurt feelings or misinterpretation. If we *are* willing to talk too often a conversation bully is looming nearby. If a conversation starts heating up and you find yourself steaming with it, take a moment before you lash out. Reflexive anger will subside if you can pause for a few seconds. If the temperature is rising, cool it off by lightening up the mood with a joke or changing the subject for a few minutes. If that doesn't work, then it's time to end the conversation and you may want to apply the *Ticking Box* approach.

Reflexive Anger: An automatic reaction of anger without conscious thought.

Why is this Brown Box Ticking?

So you were in the middle of a polite conversation when suddenly things took a turn for the explosively political. It's easy to feel flustered or angry in those situations. Reflexive anger can often be the culprit. This is when your natural instinct kicks in and you simply react. Someone suddenly loses their temper and your anger instinctively shows up. The best thing you can do is stop the conversation before something goes KABOOM. Take a deep breath and fall back on the two pillars of Cheerfulness and Respect. "Bob, I need to stop this conversation. I am very careful about how I discuss certain topics and we've wandered into a dangerous area we don't need to be in." It is possible that 'Bob' feels the exact same way and will welcome the chance to change the subject. If he doesn't, then regardless of 'Bob's' reaction, you transform yourself into a welcoming host/hostess and cheerfully change the subject. Cheerfully does not mean you turn into a Barbie or Ken Doll. Cheerfully means good grace and a clean heart. So, no wishing him dead, no planning to say nasty things behind his back. Accept that things took an unexpected turn for the worse and that you are making a necessary course correction. Regardless of 'Bob's' attitude when it's over, let it be over. Avoid allowing bad behavior on someone else's part to justify bad behavior on yours.

Skeptics welcome. Cynics need not apply
Shutting Down Darth Vader

Below are merely suggestions to get the ball rolling. The goal is to shut them down and make them go away. Preparing in advance to deal with the experts, the political junkies and the self proclaimed pros will find you triumphant. Be consistent in your attempts and they WILL go away.

Political Bullies. Go ahead and despise their behavior. They are rude, selfish and decidedly un-American. They don't care about civil discourse they only care about being right... and they are right no matter what. I looked it up and the technical term for these people is Goobers. Goobers do not deserve your time, your effort or your emotional investment. They should be dumped like radioactive waste. There are a million things to say to stop their chatter. Here are just a few:

- You're opinion has been heard
- Our conversation is over
- Your behavior is disrespectful
- Nonetheless
- I don't share your opinions
- I don't accept your premise so let's change the subject
- Your words are not appreciated
- Please keep that to yourself, thank you
- Your behavior has ended this conversation
- A person convinced against his will is of the same opinion still

Put them in your own words and do your best to use them as a shield, not a sword. Be certain you are respectful and polite... because the moral high ground is the most satisfying place to be! When someone treats you like dirt and you correct them in a classy way they are twice embarrassed. Pitching at the dirt they are lobbing only gives their argument weight and meaning. Since that kind of behavior and demeanor says way more about them than it does about you, let it go. The best thing you can do is say just enough and then be silent. They deserve a big piece of your mind, but it only plays into their prejudice and cynicism. Disallow their opinion to matter and you'll have them stewing for the rest of the day. They are cynics, the very definition of a closed mind.

Political Junkies

These people can be some of the coolest and alternatively worst humans on the planet. They might be well informed and enjoy talking about all things political, or they might be a party faithful spending all of their time gathering sound bites and speculation to 'share' with unsuspecting people. The best way to deal with the closed minded variety is to let them spin themselves out. This is an enjoyable process, because most self proclaimed junkies have very little actual knowledge. They also have very few supported, well founded personal opinions. Do not challenge them to an argument, because that's what they want. Instead, let them share their vast knowledge on a topic... because they usually have none. Rarely is a Political Junkie more than 3 questions deep.

They have strong opinions and lots of sound bites, but they don't actually know what they are talking about. So ask them to explain their upset. When they spout a sound bite, ask them where they heard it and the context in which it was said. Ask them what else they know that supports the argument. Ask them what they have read. If they cite a study or a poll ask who's study? Who's poll? Who paid for the study? Without ever having to go a single round with the junkies, you can beat them at their own game. Just give them enough rope to hang themselves and they'll do the rest.

Anyone Can Be a Firefighter

Staying calm in the heat of the moment is crucial to self preservation. Saying angry things or reacting with an extreme emotion will only fuel a fire that you are better served by putting out.

Sometimes things go badly no matter what you do. Respect is a permanent fixture, but sometimes cheerful will fall by the wayside in order to shut someone down. Someone may be angry or feel hurt that you stopped a conversation, but that is not your problem. Your focus is on keeping welcome conversations in your space and unwelcome ones out. Whatever someone's motive, if the conversation becomes an unwelcome one you have the right to shut it down. As long as you were respectful, the upset of the person who crossed the line is his/her own fault. Maybe next time that person will think harder before behaving badly towards others. Certainly they will think twice before putting you in the crosshairs again. Bullies always travel along the path of least resistance and you just became effort.

Parting words on Talking Politics:

Decisions that affect our lives and the world we live in are topics worth talking about. They come cloaked in this charged word we call Politics. This word has no power and should not stop you from talking about things that are important to you and your life.

You should feel free to have an open exchange of ideas in a safe place. Find the right people and when you do:

- Respectfully Facilitate
- Be Thoughtful
- Stay Balanced
- Put Out Fires
- Don't React – Respond
- Run a quick 'Respect Check'
- Be Cheerful or Pleasant
- When Necessary: Diffuse, Detach and Disassociate

Definitions

Absentee Ballot: A ballot submitted by mail before an election by a voter who is unable to come to the polls in person.

Adjourn: Stop a meeting with the intention of coming back to it later.

Advocacy Group: A pressure group, normally set up for a specific political aim.

Alien: A person residing under a government or in a country other than that of one's birth without citizenship.

Amendment: A proposal by a Member (in committee or floor session of the respective Chamber) to change the language or provisions of a bill or act. It is voted on in the same manner as a bill.

Apathetic Voters (The way people in the know view it): Those who have a lack of interest, enthusiasm or concern and shirk their patriotic and civic duty.

Apathetic Voters (The way I view it): Hopeful Americans who have been dismissed from government and/or feel excluded from the political process.

Appoint: To Assign a job or a role.

Autonomy: Independence or freedom; the right of self-government.

Ballot: The voting paper for a typically secret vote.

Bicameral: Made up of 2 chambers.

Bill: A written document that suggests a new law.

Bill of Rights: The first ten amendments to the US Constitution, ratified in 1791 guaranteeing such rights as the freedoms of speech, assembly, and worship.

Cabinet: Is traditionally made up of the Vice President and the heads of 15 executive departments.

Campaign Trail: Planned events in different places that are taken part in or given by a candidate who is trying to be elected.

Carry a state: To win the state.

Checks and Balances: A system that allows each branch of a government to change or veto acts of another branch to prevent any one branch from becoming too powerful.

Chamber: a legislative, judicial, or other like body

Citizen: A native or naturalized member of a state or nation.

Civil Rights movement: A worldwide political movement for equality under the law.

Commander-in-Chief: A head of state or officer in supreme command of a country's military.

Concurrent Powers: Duties shared by both the national government and state governments, such as collecting taxes, building roads, and making/enforcing laws.

Confirmation: Action by the Senate approving Presidential nominees for the executive branch, regulatory commissions, and certain other positions.

Congress: The legislative body of the U.S.

Constitution: A document that embodies the fundamental laws and principles by which the United States is governed.

Convene: To call people together.

Corporate Lobbying: When the corporations and firms try to influence business and government leaders to create legislation or conduct an activity that will help their organization.

Definitions

Corruption: An official has been influenced by a bribe of money or gifts to do something illegal.

Counterfeiting: Making illegal and fake money on purpose to deceive a person or agency.

Decennial: Occurring every ten years.

Declaration of Independence: At the Second Continental Congress, a comitte of five men drafted a document stating that the 13 colonies were officially its own country, free from English laws. All people have rights that no one should take away. A version written mostly by Thomas Jefferson was accepted on July 4, 1775.

Delegate: A representative to a convention or a conference, such as the Constitutional Convention.

Democrat: An advocate of democracy (a government by the people), believing in the political or social equality of all people. They are generally considered to be 'liberal' or 'left-wing.' The Donkey represents this group.

Democratic National Committee (DNC): Provides national leadership for the Democratic Party of the United States. It is responsible for developing and promoting the Democratic political platform, as well as coordinating fundraising and election strategy.

Democratic Party: The party is considered to be liberal. It is represented by the donkey and the color blue.

Democratic: Political or social equality for all.

Diplomat: Someone who is skilled in negotiating between nations without making any of the nations angry.

Districts: States are divided into sections of territory. Each section of territory is permitted one U.S. Congressperson to represent the people in that section of territory in the U.S. House of Representatives.

Donkey: This animal represents the Democratic Party.

Early voting: The process by which electors can vote on a single or series of days prior to an election. It can take place remotely, such as by mail, or in person, usually in designated early voting polling places.

Economy: Wealth and resources in terms of the production and consumption of goods and services.

Election: Is a formal decision making process by which a population chooses an individual to hold public office.

Elector: A member of the Electoral College.

Electoral Math: Adding up the electoral votes of the states you think you can win in to see if you have 270 of them.

Elephant: This animal represents the Republican Party.

Enrolled Bill: A copy of a bill passed by both houses of Congress, signed by their presiding officers, and sent to the President for signature.

Exploratory Committee: A group created to help decide if a potential candidate should run.

FAIR: Fairness and accuracy in reporting.

Federal Communications Commission (FCC): An independent government agency that regulates interstate and international communications by radio, television, wire, cable, and satellite.

Federal Election Commission (FEC): An independent regulatory agency that makes sure candidates obey the law when they raise and spend money for their campaigns.

Fiscal Policies: A government course of action for dealing with the budget (particularly with taxation and borrowing).

Definitions

Founding Fathers: The delegates to the Constitutional Convention who established the basis of American government.

Framers: This title refers to the men who put together the U.S. Constitution.

Front Runner: The candidate that is leading in the race.

Gaffe: An unintentional remark causing embarrassment to its originator; a blunder.

General Election: A regular election of candidates for office, as opposed to a primary election.

Government: The way we are together. A body that makes and enforces laws in a society.

Great Depression: This began in 1929 and lasted until the 1940's. During this time businesses and banks closed their doors; people lost their jobs, homes and savings; and many depended on charity to survive.

Green: A political party whose policies are based on concern for the environment.

Grievance: The formal expression of a charge of injustice against a person or persons.

Hard Money: Money given directly to a candidate in an election to assist his or her campaign.

Head of Government: Describes either the highest or second highest official in the executive branch of a sovereign state, a federated state, or a self-governing colony who often presides over a cabinet.

Head of State: The chief public representative of a country who may also be the head of the government.

Hearing: A meeting or session of a committee of Congress, usually open to the public, to obtain information and opinions on proposed legislation, conduct an investigation, or oversee a program.

Hook: That thing or piece of information that draws people in. It can also highlight the type of candidate they are going to run as – the "progressive candidate.' "The Moderate," "The Conservative" and so on.

House Bill: A bill originating in the U.S. House of Representatives.

Ideology: A set of ideas that makes up a person's goals, expectations, and actions.

Immigrant: A person who migrates to another country, usually for permanent residence.

Impeach: A process that is used to charge, try, and remove public officials for misconduct while in office.

Inauguration: The act of formally introducing an official into public office.

Independent: Not part of any formal political party or ideology.

Joint Resolution: A resolution passed by both houses of Congress.

Judicial: The branch of government that tries cases and decides if laws are constitutional. It is led by the Supreme Court.

Judicial Review: The power of a court to judge the constitutionality of the laws of a government or the acts of a government official.

Justice: One of nine members of the Supreme Court.

Lame duck: An elected official who is serving out the time between an election and the inauguration of a replacement.

Landslide: An election won by a large majority of the votes cast.

Definitions

Legislative: The branch of our government with the power to make the laws.

Libertarian: With diverse beliefs, an advocate of strict limits to government activity and sharing the goal of maximizing individual liberty and political freedom.

Likely voters: Registered voters believed to be committed to casting their vote.

Line-Item Veto: The power of the executive to disapprove of particular items of a bill without having to disapprove of the entire bill.

Moderator: The person running a debate.

National Convention: A convention of a major political party, especially one that nominates a candidate for the presidency.

Partisanship: Showing favoritism to one's own party.

Platform: A document stating the goals and principles of a political party.

Pocket Veto: A veto of a bill brought about by an indirect rejection by the president. The president is granted ten days, Sundays excepted, to review a piece of legislation passed by Congress. Should he fail to sign a piece of legislation and Congress has adjourned within those ten days, the bill is automatically killed.

Politic: Shrewd or prudent in practical matters; tactful; diplomatic.

Political: Of, pertaining to, or concerned with politics.

Political Campaign: A race between candidates for elective office.

Political Climate: The change in mood and opinions of the people about political issues.

Political Convention: A formal meeting of members, representatives, or delegates of a political party.

Political party: A group of people wanting to take hold of power or influence government policy, usually by nominating their own candidates and trying to seat them in political office. There are typically 2 political parties in the United States, the Republicans and Democrats.

Political Philosophy: Usually refers to a general view, or specific ethic, belief or attitude, about politics.

Politics: The science or art of Political government. The practice or profession of conducting political affairs.

Polling Place: A building where voting takes place during an election.

Pollsters: The folks who conduct polls to get data on everything from testing the validity of the candidate's message to finding out which color jacket he/she should wear to appear the most trustworthy.

Preside: Be in charge of or be in the position of authority in a meeting or gathering.

President of the United States: Head of the Executive Branch. The president's power is dictated by the Constitution.

Presidential line of succession: The United States presidential line of succession defines who may become or act as President of the United States upon the incapacity, death, resignation, or removal from office (by impeachment and subsequent conviction) of a sitting president or a president-elect.

Primary Election: An election held to decide which candidates will be on the November general election ballot.

Propose: To put forward an idea or plan for consideration.

Definitions

Provisional Ballot: A "fail-safe" enacted by congress requiring election officials to provide this special ballot to individuals who are being denied the vote for some reason. Once the appropriate election officials determine the individual is eligible to vote, the ballot is counted. In many cases an eligible ballot is not counted.

Public Law: A bill or joint resolution (other than for amendments to the Constitution) passed by both Houses of Congress and approved by the President. Bills and joint resolutions vetoed by the President, but overridden by the Congress also become public law.

Pundit: A person who gives opinions in an authoritative manner usually through the mass media: Critic.

Ratify: to make something legal by signing it or giving formal consent.

Recession: A period of decline in the growth of the economy.

Redistricting: The process within the States of redrawing legislative district boundaries to reflect population changes following the decennial census.

Referendum: The submission of a law, proposed or already in effect, to a direct vote of the people.

Report: The printed record of a committee's actions, including its votes, recommendations, and views on a bill or question of public policy or its findings and conclusions based on oversight inquiry, investigation, or other study.

Republic: A state or nation in which the supreme power rests in all the citizens entitled to vote and is exercised by representatives elected, directly or indirectly, by them and responsible to them.

Republican: An advocate of a limited role of the Federal Government in solving the problems of society. The elephant represents this group. They are also referred to as the G.O.P. (Grand Old Party) and are generally considered to be 'conservative' or 'right-wing.'

Resolution: A firm decision to do or not to do something

Senators: Members of the Senate who were elected by their state. Their job is to make laws, and they serve 6 year terms.

Simple Resolution: In the United States, a simple resolution is a legislative measure passed by either the Senate or the House of Representatives.

Soft Money: Political donations made in such a way as to avoid federal regulations or limits, as by donating to a party organization rather than to a particular candidate or campaign.

Sound Bite: A brief, striking remark or statement excerpted from an audiotape or videotape for insertion in a broadcast news story. A short extract from a recorded interview, chosen for its pungency or appropriateness.

Sovereign: Above or superior to all others; chief; greatest; supreme dominion or power.

Special Interest Group: Is a group with an interest in advancing solutions to issues. They may at times also advocate or lobby on a particular issue or on a range of issues.

Spin: To provide an interpretation of a statement or event, especially in a way meant to sway public opinion.

State Election Office/State board of elections: A body designated to conduct elections in a state.

State Party Convention: A party meeting held every two years for the purpose of nominating candidates.

Super Tuesday: A day on which a large group of U.S. States hold their primary elections.

Supreme Court: The highest federal court in the United States. It takes precedence over all other courts in the nation.

Definitions

Swing States (or Battleground States): States where the two major political parties have about the same levels of support among voters, and are also viewed as important in determining the overall result of a presidential election.

The Republican National Committee (RNC): Provides national leadership for the Republican Party of the United States. It is responsible for developing and promoting the Republican political platform, as well as coordinating fundraising and election strategy.

Treaties: A formal agreement between two or more states.

Undecideds: People who have not declared a party nor have they decided on who they will vote for.

Unlikely voters: Those who are eligible to vote, but aren't registered and are believed to be uninterested in voting.

Veto: A vote that blocks a decision made by law makers.

Voting: A formal expression of your opinion or your choice.

Whip: An official in a political party whose primary purpose is to party discipline. They threaten punishments for party members to make them vote according to the official party policy.

Me The People

Sources and Resources

To track down all of this information there was lots of stuff I did: Places I went, people I talked to, articles I read, things I watched and websites I surfed.

Some Books and Magazines I used

Bowers, Jennifer. American Education Publishing. School Specialty P, 2000.

Cox, Ana Marie. (2007, February 26). How Big Money Picks a Winner. Time Magazine.

Duffy, Micheal. (2006, November 6). Can This Machine Be Trusted? Time Magazine.

Goodman, Susan and Smith, Elwood. See How They Run, Campaign Dreams, Election Schemes, and the Race to the White House. Bloomsbury Children's Books, 2008.

Greenberg, Ellen. The House and Senate Explained, the People's Guide to Congress. W.W. Norton and Company, 1996.

Kenneday, Senator Edward. My Senator and Me. New York, Scholastic Press, 2006.

Shenkman, Rick. Just How Stupid Are We? Facing the Truth About the American Voter. Basic Books, 2008.

Von Oech, Roger. A Kick in the Seat of the Pants. Harper Perennial, 1986.

Von Oech, Roger. A Whack on the Side of the Head, How You Can be More Creative. Warner Books, 1983.

Additional Websites

www.USgovinfor.About.com   www.BensGuide.gpo.gov

Movies and DVDs

West Wing: I can't say enough about how much you can learn while vegging in front of the TV to this award winning show. It takes place at the White House and brings you behind the scenes to the inner workings of government, politics and the lives of public servants. It's smart, it's funny and it's a chance to learn a lot about the Executive and Legislative branches without having to crack open a stale book. And hey, you can't go wrong with Rob Lowe, Allison Janney or Martin Sheen!

Game Change: This factual fictional film about the 2008 Presidential Election is a fast paced inside look at politics and the reality of Presidential campaigns, campaigning and the humanness of the people who run. It is both fascinating and entertaining.

Thank You!

I want to give my thanks to the dozens of people who offered their points of view and perspective. Specifically, I thank the people who bravely shared their ignorance and their fears about government and politics. Their openness helped me include information we'd all find useful.

Top Bananas

Sara Manzano-Diaz, Director of the Women's Bureau, U.S. Department of Labor – For encouraging me to put this guide together.

Dave Davis, Director of State and Local Relations at Northwestern University – For his commitment to helping people.

Jan Schakowsky, U.S. Congresswoman, Washington D.C. – For giving *Me, The People* the Congressional Thumbs Up!

Ken Bennett, Regional Representative of US Secretary of Labor, U.S. Department of Labor – For thinking that sharing this kind of information was a good idea and saying so.

Sources And Resources

Melanie Becker, Federal Highway Administration, Program Analyst; Washington, DC– For sharing practical advice along the way.

Dr. Azza Layton, Professor of Political Science, DePaul University – For graciously contributing her expertise.

Jonathan Williams, Manager Community Services, Office of Cook County Clerk David Orr, Election Division – For his enthusiastic and comprehensive efforts to involve the community in politics and government.

Jack Canfield, Breakthrough to Success – For his unending efforts towards teaching people how to design the joyous life they desire.

Particular thanks to **County Supervisor Linda Langston of Iowa** (Linn County Supervisor of District 2, First Vice President of NACo (Nat'l Assoc of Counties)), and the Langston family. I was generously welcomed into their home and offered exclusive access into the political world. This book is here for you because they were there for me.

A very special thanks to David Blake, who helped prove that becoming more politically aware, politically involved and governmentally savvy CAN be fun, fast and easy!